SIS

WITH POWER

Edited by

BISHOP JOE ALDRED

*To Hyacinth from the Golden
Agers
God bless you

Joe A*

CONTINUUM
London and New York

Continuum

The Tower Building, 11 York Road, London SE1 7NX

370 Lexington Avenue, New York, NY 10017-6503

First published 2000

British Library Cataloguing-in-Publication Data
A catalogue record for this book is available from the British Library.

ISBN 0–8264–9985–9

Typeset by Kenneth Burnley, Wirral, Cheshire.
Printed and bound in Great Britain by
The Guernsey Press Co. Ltd, Guernsey, C.I.

CONTENTS

INTRODUCTION

This book is a first! The first collection of writings by a majority black, but also including Asian and white, Christian women from across the British church scene. This work is the result of a commitment by the Centre for Black and White Christian Partnership to actualize Christian unity and reconciliation between the various cultural and denominational expressions of the Christian faith co-existing in the UK. The Centre acknowledges that there are imbalances and inequalities that get in the way of true Christian unity and is therefore committed to engage in the struggle for a unity based on mutual respect between legitimate cultural and denominational Christian faith expressions. A three-pronged approach is adopted for this interdenominational, intercultural Christian ministry of reconciliation. First, a commitment to raise awareness to the prevalence of racism in society and the Christian Church. Second, a commitment to work towards the empowerment of the weak and disadvantaged, and those who are willing to engage in the struggle for the realization of Christian unity in diversity. Third, a commitment to bring about meaningful engagement between Asian, Black and White Christians in Britain. The Centre pursues its goals in a number of ways, and this compilation is one of those ways.

A tragedy of our time is that some cultures, in particular black cultures, are pigeonholed, stigmatized even, as 'oral'; while others, in particular white European cultures, are regarded as 'literary'. Clearly, all cultures enjoy both elements in their tradition to some extent. However, an unfortunate, if inevitable, result of this stereotyping is that black cultures in Britain are not encouraged to write: the literary white cultures have traditionally written for and about them. This collection challenges this paradigm. It provides the opportunity for literary expression by a group that endures double exclusion as black and women. Hence, the majority of women in this collection are black. This is a deliberate positive action statement!

This collection is a tool of literary engagement. These Christian women present their arguments, stories and statements to the British mainstream, and further afield. Whether the reader is a lecturer, teacher or student, these women invite critical use of their material. You will be aware that you are engaging with articulate women who are speaking for themselves directly with you. No attempt has been made to edit what these women want to say: the Centre has simply provided the medium through which they speak.

Sisters with Power brings together Black, Asian and White Christian reflections on a range of topics that these women writers have chosen. The book is not topically thematic: its theme is women, mainly black women, speaking and writing for themselves. In a patriarchal society, it is matriarchal power at its best!

Yvette Hutchinson insightfully probes the notion – for some the reality – that being a woman is never enough. Often the woman is the willing, even forced, worker whose generous self-giving, over and above what is reasonable (note her use of the *braata* as symbolic of this) simply courts further demands. Giving too much becomes the expected norm! Hutchinson concludes that women, by their over-generosity, create a rod for their own backs. For her, women have given, and are, more than enough.

Kate Coleman adopts an autobiographical approach to examine many of the issues related to being a black, single Christian woman. She argues that human wholeness and God-centredness are key to the single life. Citing examples of singleness such as Jesus, she argues that singleness is in fact the original state of all and should never be seen as a lower state than being married: just different. Coleman introduces us to the highs and lows, challenges and privileges of being a single black woman, and in her case a minister too.

Mukti Barton launches a robust challenge to oppressive patriarchy in the Church. She demonstrates how a male-orientated reading of the Bible and application of hermeneutics have obscured the contribution of the many women, including many black women, in the scriptures. Barton believes passionately that God is on the side of the marginalized, poor and oppressed and, as Jesus demonstrated in his ministry, is on the side of women who have been and are oppressed, marginalized and made poor by men.

Dionne Lamont, in similar vein to Barton, critiques male supremacy in the Church, its androcentric and misogynist tendencies in traditional theology and biblical interpretation. Lamont demands women's right to the privilege of leadership at all levels in the Church. She refutes the notion that male gender hegemony can take precedence over Christians being one in Christ, whether they are male, female, black, white, Jew or Gentile.

Lorraine Dixon discusses her own challenges in response to her calling to the ministry. She wrestles with the possible parallels between the historic absurdities of enslavement subjugation and a calling to become a deacon as a black woman in a majority white British Church. Dixon brings into view some of the womanist paradigms that have helped and are helping her to develop her own ministry as a deacon.

Angela Sarkis presents the case for acknowledgement of the unique contribution that has been made by women towards the development of society. The professional woman is something of a rarity among black British women, but a growing aspect of life in Britain today. Sarkis posits some of the dilemmas faced by such people, in attempting to be a professional in the workplace, and wife, mother, auntie, carer, friend and lover. She offers some helpful tips, as a mentor, to aspirants and experienced operators, about how to own and pursue professional goals.

Christine Russell Lumby offers glimpses from her experience, as well as theories from professionals in the field, on leadership. She contrasts qualities found in female and male leaders, focusing particularly upon the up-sides and down-sides of the woman leader. Russell Lumby encourages women to forge alliances where appropriate with male colleagues in their challenge to female subjugation, whether in church or secular work. She also offers some biblical models for resistance.

Janet Johnson uses poetic language to describe her Jesus encounter and life as a woman in the Church. She traces her journey of cultural and spiritual discovery and the points of connection with her roots. Johnson describes her discovery of black studies and black theology as rebirth: being born again, this time in a world in which being black is valued and nurtured.

Sandra Ackroyd shares with the reader a personal story about life as a minister's wife. A wife, yes, but a woman with her own hopes, aspirations and ambitions who has to learn the skill of balancing her expectations with those of others. Ackroyd's story is one of a successful forging of a ministry that was true to her calling. She helps the reader to understand how one woman learned and applied practical rules of engagement in the parsonage while living in the world, in and out of the Church.

Hyacinth Sweeney is concerned with the problematic nature of the Bible for women, whilst attempting to use it as the word of God and a tool for growth. She outlines how some ordinary people and theologians have developed their own canons by a process of selectivization of biblical texts. Sweeney understands this re-canonization as an historic and ongoing process in black homes and churches.

Muriel Mohabir emphasizes the divine origin of the design that a woman is. She offers a robust assertion that woman is God's creation, made in his image, the co-equal of the man. Mohabir stresses the uniqueness of the woman and some of her attributes and roles. Whilst the woman shares some qualities with man, she is different in important ways: not inferior, just different. She offers some tips on how to accentuate woman-hood in the face of visible and invisible opposition.

Pauline Muir utilizes the 'virtuous woman' of Proverbs 31 as a paradigm for modern womanist virtuosity. She uses it to illustrate a radical feminism that is based upon the biblical principles found there and applied to the contemporary twenty-first-century context. Muir challenges the modern Christian woman to not become bound by societal (including church) restrictions; to shake off the 'Can't do' and get into the 'Can do' mode that is consistent with her paradigm.

Andrea Encinas-Meade announces the death of the myth of the strong black woman. The woman that features in the opening chapter of this book is, according to Meade, officially dead – the one who lives for and by other people's expectations even at the cost of her own personal unfulfilment and demise. The enduring, set-up-to-fail, exploited-by-sexism-and-racism-woman has died and in her place has resurrected the overcoming and transforming black woman. She is free from pretence, independent of over-expectation, accepting of difference, frank and vulnerable!

Nicola Tavares-Mott closes this work with poetry that is refreshingly clever, honest, hard hitting and thought provoking. Her work provides a fitting conclusion to what is a quite absorbing collection of work by women in British church life today.

As rich and powerful as this collection is, my experience of bringing these writers together in this volume is that they represent only the tip of an iceberg. Britain's churches are awash with talent, and it is hoped that appearing here will simply be the push that some of these and other women need to write more. The sobering truth is that if you do not write your own story, others will write it for and about you! The best witness is surely the eye-witness:

We proclaim to you what we have seen and heard, so that you also may have fellowship with us. And our fellowship is with the Father and with his Son, Jesus Christ. We write this to make our joy complete. (1 John 1:3–4, NIV)

The project simply would not have happened without the administrative support of Donna Gordon-Rowe. She has given her time and talents as a volunteer at great cost to herself. We all owe her the uttermost gratitude. Donna has given herself in this way because she believes in the project, in the need to give women more literary voice. It is not that women do not have a voice, just that a male-dominated world often blocks it out of mainstream. Donna has helped to apply this limited corrective. Once again, a big 'Thank you'! Appreciation is due also to Nicola Balkham at the Centre office and Colleen Laing who helped us out at the end. All the contributors have done their work as a labour of love, and I thank them on all our behalfs for enriching our lives with their words.

Enjoy! Stay blessed!

BISHOP JOE ALDRED

Executive Director

Centre for Black and White Christian Partnership

March 2000

WHEN BEING A WOMAN IS NOT ENOUGH

Yvette Hutchinson

Yvette Hutchinson works in Education Management and is an Asso-
ciate Lecturer in Post-Colonial Literature for the Open University.
She is committed to a 'socially and politically active' Christian faith
and attends a 'post-Brethren' evangelical chapel. Yvette is completing
her PhD studies in Black Culture and Arts.

Of course, when they ask for poems about the 'realities' of
black women,
>
> What they really want
> at times is a specimen
> whose heart is in the dust.
>
> A mother-of sufferer
> trampled, oppressed
> they want a little black blood
> undressed
> and validation
> for the abused stereotype
> already in their heads.
>
> Or else they want
> a perfect song. (Nichols, 1989, p. 52)

Like Nichols, in recognizing the spectrum of black women's
identities, I am loath to present any one image as unilateral
reality. I could say that being a woman is not *seen* as enough and
as expectations increase, so do the psychological and emotional
dangers for black women. I could extol the virtues of black
mothers and sisters everywhere who give unceasingly to the
communities of the family, friendship and church. I could cite
popular music and fiction to illustrate the significance of the

1

Superwoman complex, our need of it and our benefits from it. I could also cite the stories of black women whose experiences are positive, empowering and community-based. There are others whose lives are centred outside close community networks, who thrive in non-Christian spiritual purpose and live wholesome, productive lives. There is a significant body of anecdotal, telephonic, diaried and 'shared-over-dinner' evidence to support all of these statements. There is a smaller body of academic and research material, but hopefully collections like this will work to remedy that situation.

When I was invited to submit a chapter for this collection, I was struck by the title because it could be read in a variety of ways. Loving a challenge, I chose to regard the title as 'having the plantation on its back'[1] with the usual causative continuum: black woman = struggle = thankless task, but 'thank God for Jesus'. Having imposed this reading on the title, it then made it easier for me to challenge assumptions that are anathema to my own perspective, to how I choose to view the world and to the way the models in my life encouraged me to think. While I recognize therefore that I have chosen a particular reading of 'enough', it is still fair to suggest that this reading is sufficiently common and prevalent among black people to warrant discussion.

The preoccupation about the sufficiency of being a woman is one that I would suggest does not occupy the minds of men about themselves. To suggest that one's essential being and gender identity is not enough can be both a sacrilegious challenge to God's handiwork and evidence of the way in which society negates women in their very essence. One can only guess at the effect of this idea of insufficiency on women in general and black women in particular. I wonder what it is about being a woman that is not enough? Equally, I am curious about who decides what is enough. Is it God, ourselves, our parents, our children, our partners, our bosses . . . ? There is a variety of ways in which it could be argued that being a woman is not enough. In a society that lauds the role of the wife and mother but makes it very difficult for a woman to stay at home and fulfil those roles, a woman is never doing enough, either as a wife or mother.

In the working world, a woman who is committed to her career is constrained to limit her choices regarding her domestic and personal life. She has to prove her worth to her colleagues and defend her choices to her family and friends. For the majority of women, either as working mothers in relationships, single mothers on their own, or indeed, single women, the binary infrastructure for career and/or family is unyielding and in itself not enough. I have chosen therefore to tussle with the concept of 'enough' and sufficiency and to offer a subversive reading of black women and being enough.

From a Christian perspective men and women are taught to seek insufficiency and strive to be the hollow shell that is quickened by the indwelling of God's Holy Spirit. 'Letting go and letting God' allows the individual to yield to the omniscient patronage of God. To recognize one's own weakness in the face of God's omnipotence is the first step in the relationship between the individual and the Godhead. At the same time, it could be argued, such submission allows for the abrogation of personal responsibility to one's self and to one's political and social obligations. There is a fine balance between the strength and power that a relationship with God endows and one's own powerlessness. To revel in one's own incapacity can move from a healthy dependence on God to a lazy approach to oneself and the world. Thus, as Christians we can be accused, rightly in some cases, of fiddling while our communities burn with dysfunctional relationships and the effects of substance abuse; of having watched on the sidelines as the result of institutionalized discrimination continuously replays itself in the economic and social structures of our communities. 'Letting go and letting God' has left many of us without the ability to apply the truths of our faith in a meaningful way with and among our people.

As black women we take inspiration from that famous verse in Philippians 4:13: 'I can do everything through him who gives me strength' and feed our children, support our families and thrive. We dance to the tune of our ability in his strength but always hear the counterpoint that incants 'He must become greater; I must become less' (John 3:30, NIV). Yielding to God and the advice to submit to men in the church and the home, black

3

women are burdened with entreaties to submissive service. Black Christian women daily experience the dichotomy between the striving for the sublimation of self that is part of the Christian journey and the black women's historical journey which has been for the expression of self and identity. While it is not the purview of this discussion to consider issues of identity and understanding of self for Christians whose identity, according to many doctrinal teachings, must be subsumed under the largesse of God's love, those concerns must inform the ways in which black women negotiate a sense of self in relation to God, in response to the racist patriarchal strictures of the occidental world, and in relation to their partners, families and friends.

What we expect from God is more than sufficient. What we expect must be all-encompassing from the God who, we have been told, 'is able to do immeasurably more than all we ask or imagine' (Ephesians 3:20, NIV). Our expectations of the 'Servant King' are unquestioning. We depend on the sufficiency of God to take us through the minutiae of our daily lives. The mother heart of God prepares the way for us and organizes our lives in this earthly realm. We are charged with the responsibility to replicate this selfless love and giving in our relationships and to give without ceasing.

Certainly from a Caribbean perspective, it is expected that black women are nurturers, sharers and replenishers. Particularly for diasporan peoples, the mother/woman role is to create a haven for the displaced. That haven needs to make provision for physical, social and psychological needs. It is a mark of pride for a black woman to be intelligent, ambitious, supportive and yet 'traditional'. These expectations are further strengthened by biblical teaching to give one to another and to love others as ourselves. And yet, very often black women are giving more than we would give to ourselves; giving primary care and nurture to others before acknowledging our own needs, sometimes denying our own struggles in order to support our black brothers in their quest for greater professional recognition, coyly dismissing our own achievements in order to spare the feelings of others.[2] There is a continuum of giving that begins with less self and ends with selfless. This can be identified in two ways:

first, as already discussed, in the negation of self for the ultimate manifestation of God in our lives. Second, this selflessness can mean the diminishing of the black woman and her personal needs for the greater good of family and community. The sad irony is that it is in the diminishing self that the black woman is finally 'enough' and her contribution of any significance. Complicit in our own destruction, in this continuum we strive for selflessness to our personal, psychological and professional detriment. The notion of sufficient or enough then becomes a nonsense in that the gradations of selflessness approach self-destructive heights.

We are taught that Jesus died for our sins, died that we no longer have to die, and rose again that we could be victorious. Yet many of us thrive, living on the giving and selflessness that is bought at the price of a diminished black woman. Our expectations are such that we have lost the ability to recognize when enough and more than enough has been sacrificed for our comfort. One cannot appreciate the 'extra', or the *braata* as we say in Jamaica, if the expectations are that one always gets from black women who must always give.

The *braata* is that extra something; it is a gift, an honorarium, it is over and above that which is required. Indeed the *braata* is 'immeasurably more than all we ask or imagine'. It is immeasurable not in terms of quantity, even though that too can be the case, but in terms of the kindness and the thoughtfulness of the act itself. *Braata* is an independent act of kindness and a transaction, it is a statement about the relationship between the giver and the recipient.

In my consideration of 'when being a woman is not enough' I will use *braata* as a paradigm that acknowledges black women's sufficiency and our consistent demonstration of 'more than enough' in all aspects of our lives.

An excellent example of *braata* can be observed in markets all over the Caribbean. Country women selling their agricultural produce are wary of the disdainful shopper who bruises fruit and questions the sweetness of the orange, the freshness of the callaloo and the juiciness of the lime. There is a sophisticated ritual where the vendor and customer decide whether to cajole or 'cuss'; to begin a slanging match or expedite a cold transaction. If cajoling takes place, then the customer needs to respect the quality of the vendor's produce and the vendor, in turn, needs to acknowledge the unerring percipience of the customer in coming to the stall with the finest produce. There are distinct power dynamics in such a transaction and the *braata* – which can be an extra lime, a generously weighed bunch of callalloo – may be withheld. *Braata* is an extra and is bestowed on the worthy; one has the power to endow the *braata* but the silver-tongued or the desperate cannot elicit *braata*. *Braata* is more than just the extra fruit in the bag, it is also a blessing; *braata* is good words and good wishes and beyond the rituals of mere barter. My primary example of *braata* has been commercial and relating to commodity, but *braata* should not be limited in this way. Indeed as a blessing and goodwill, *braata* is at its most meaningful away from the commercial arena, when it is placed within the context of human relations.

Braata is shared and represents a relationship between people. This can happen between strangers and when it does it offers the beginnings of a relationship. *Braata* blesses the giver and the recipient. In bestowing *braata* you recognize that you have extended yourself on behalf of someone else. The ability to do that is in itself a blessing. As black women, in whom 'giving' has been inculcated from youth, we are fulfilling our purpose when we successfully serve others and bless them in our giving. *Braata* is precious because we can choose to bestow it, it can be an expression of faith and the sealing of trust. To be meaningful *braata* must be sacrificial, it must go beyond reasonable duty and expectation.

It is hoped that this extension of the self is recognized by the recipient, not to gain praise, but because extra, more than enough, should not go unnoticed. A blessing must not be accepted with complacency but gratefully received for all it represents: kindness, thoughtfulness, trust and a prophecy of good things. I feel that I should state emphatically that *braata* is never the norm and it should not be possible for it to become so. What may happen is that as the *braata* is shared it is accepted a little too readily. As expectations increase, *braata* is no longer regarded as a sacrificial extension of the self but as the normal way of things. In many ways that is why we can discuss 'when being a woman is not enough'. Selfless, continuous giving and the over-extension of oneself countless times becomes an established pattern, so the best a black woman can do is never enough. *Braata* then becomes not a blessing but a curse because it represents the successful achievement of the highest target that must be achieved constantly. If '*braata* as the norm' were to occur, having questioned the recipient we then would have to question the giver. How did *braata* metamorphose from blessing to curse? Was *braata* squandered? Can *braata* be squandered by deed or by word? If this were possible, *braata* would become a vulgar commodification from which the essence has gone. What are the consequences of this? Who must be responsible and what will be the effects on our communities? If a squandered *braata* represents the over-extension of black women to their communities, what could this mean for their well-being? The danger would be that black women would be extending themselves beyond what is healthy and appropriate. The critic/writer bell hooks discusses this in her book *Sisters of the Yam: Black Women and Self-Recovery* (1993, pp. 55–6):

> . . . black people, and black women in particular, are so well socialized to push ourselves past healthy limits that we often do not know how to set protective boundaries that would eliminate certain forms of stress in our lives . . . In a society that socialized everyone to believe that black women were put here on this earth to be little worker bees who never stop, it is not surprising that we too have trouble calling a halt.

I am concerned that black women have trouble calling a halt; I am equally concerned that, too often, our families and friends are not willing to call a halt on our behalf. I am pained that, too often, others' greater needs allow them to commodify the *braata* that we offer. It is wrong that, too often, mothers and sister-friends judge us by our willingness to continue the gruelling pace that puts others first. It frightens me that, too often, our pastors remind us that our living, our giving, our sacrifice is not in vain for it gains us a place in heaven. It appalls me that deferred gratification is acceptable to offer to black women without a recognition of our needs here, now and in the immediate future. I am challenged that, as Sweet Honey in the Rock remind us, 'our hands are not clean'. I recognize my complicity and am ashamed.

In this exploration, I have tried to question the role of sufficiency. Rather than acceding to the popular view that being a woman is not enough, I have considered black women in their own communities as being more than enough. Black woman as representing the *braata*; a sacrificial blessing that prophesies good things, is a blessing and can, when abused, be a dreadful curse. Our lives are daily testimonies to the bestowing of *braata*, of giving, of extending ourselves and being not just sufficient, but more than enough.

During my childhood, a particularly favourite family ritual (of which there are many) was at the end of the evening meal. My mother would look proudly around the table and then ask 'Are you sufficiently sufficed?', to which my sister and I would reply, 'I'm sufficed sufficiently.'

Notes

1 I first heard this phrase in America several years ago. The writer Terri McMillan was being interviewed about her book *Waiting to Exhale* and she stated clearly that she was not carrying the plantation on her back, either in her life or in her fiction.

2 As a Jamaican woman I am fully aware of the importance of the Sunday dinner/Sufferer's Feast/Jamaica Coat of Arms. As a non-meat-eater I am always fascinated at the distribution of meat. I've observed two generations of women who always seem to be eating the wing of the chicken so the men in the family can have the tastier, meatier cuts. Every time I hear a black woman say 'It's funny you know, I prefer the neck and the wing' I wonder how long we will continue to deny ourselves and then convince ourselves that it's just how we like it?

References

hooks, bell (1993) *Sisters of the Yam: Black Women and Self-Recovery*, London: Turnaround.

Nichols, Grace (1989) 'Of course when they ask for poems about the "realities" of black women', in *Lazy Thoughts of a Lazy Woman and Other Poems*, London: Virago.

WOMAN, SINGLE, CHRISTIAN

Kate Coleman

Kate Coleman has been pastor of Chalk Farm Baptist Church for the past thirteen years. She is committed to urban mission, the ministry of women, and issues related to the black communities of Britain. She is currently studying for a PhD in Black Theology at Birmingham University. She is also a lecturer and international speaker tackling subjects such as spiritual warfare and the black presence in the Bible.

I stood with my mouth open in mute astonishment: 'She asked you to do what?' I exclaimed once again. As my pitch was a little too high, I determined to calm down. 'She asked me if I would find you a good husband', my friend said with a smile on his face.

It is not that I am averse to husbands or, in this case, averse to the idea of having one of my own. What I found alarming was that my mother, who lives in Ghana, had entrusted a courier, someone I had asked to do no more than deliver a gift while passing through my homeland, to seek out a 'suitable' man to 'complete' my life. Fortunately this 'courier' happened to be a good friend of mine. The worrying thing is that I'm not sure that my mother knew this and in any case she 'didn't know him from Adam', as the saying goes. This particular incident put me in mind of the many other couriers entrusted with bearing a gift whom 'I didn't know from Adam' (or at least I did not know very well)! It got me wondering about how many others may have been charged with similar weighty responsibilities in relation to my future happiness (or not, as the case may be).

Cultural expectations

Many who are of African or African-Caribbean descent may identify with the scenario I have just outlined. Even after lengthy stays in Britain, marriage and childbirth continue to be rites of passage into adulthood for our communities. The pressure then for some of us to marry or have children (sometimes inappropriately) can be an overwhelming one. Where I come from, single people are viewed as immature and incomplete, whether male or female. A friend of mine who didn't get married until he was well into his forties was still being referred to as a 'small boy' in spite of the fact that he had been a pastor for many years.

The prospect of visiting my homeland is usually preceded by a mixture of eager anticipation and sheer dread. My prominent position as a pastor on 'mission' usually leads to a number of responses that I inevitably have to negotiate. Those who have known me for some years continue to ask the question, 'Are you still single?' On one occasion I was introduced to a congregation of nearly 1,000 people with the words 'Please welcome Reverend Kate Coleman who is a Baptist minister in London and *still* single'. This announcement was followed by unconcealed gasps of amazement, not to mention the interest it generated among some of the young men. Similarly, those who do not know me well, if at all, also appear to be more concerned about my unmarried status than I am. There is seldom a shortage of those from both categories who feel duty bound to pray for me to find a husband (an *appropriate* one is not, it seems, always a priority).

Although I struggle with its stress on marriage and childbirth, I particularly value my cultural roots because of the emphasis they place on relationships and community; yes I even value my mother's concern for and attempts to find me 'a good man'. However, prior consultation with me as a valued member of that community would be more appreciated.

The idea that we are not islands but irreversibly interconnected such that our actions or lack of them (even in marriage, childbirth or singleness) affect one another appeals to my sense of what it means to be a human being. I am convinced that what it means to be human is manifested less through Descartes' philosophy, 'I think, therefore I am' and more through African cosmology, or as African scholar John S. Mbiti puts it, 'I am because we are, since we are, therefore I am' (1969, p. 106).

11

Genesis 1 and 2 remind us that human beings were made for community. The image of the 'Body of Christ' in the New Testament expresses a similar concern regarding individuality, interconnectedness, commitment and co-operation. Western individualism as we know it is not a feature of this new community. The attitude of the Old Testament community of faith was not unlike aspects of Ghanaian culture today. Among this ancient community there was virtually no place for single people. In the Hebrew mind, not getting married and having children was a disaster, such that the theme of being the son of a son of a son is always prominent in Old Testament texts and evidently recorded with great care. Childbirth was viewed as the sole means of continuing the family line in a context where people understood that the only afterlife they were to look forward to was 'the place of the dead', 'sheol', the grave.

Even the priests and the Nazirites were not single in this context (see Leviticus 21:1–15 and Numbers 6:1–21). Newly married men were spared the duty of warfare for their first year of marriage so that they could get to know their wives and ensure children and heirs (Deuteronomy 24:5). Barrenness was such a dreadful prospect that Genesis 16 describes the agony of Abraham's wife, Sarah, over not being able to conceive an heir for Abraham. Genesis 25:21 describes how Isaac prayed for his wife Rebekah to conceive. In Genesis 30:1 Rachel says to Jacob 'Give me children, or I'll die' and so it continues, except that there is also another theme to be found in the Old Testament record. Through this alternative theme God seemingly counters this obsession with marriage and childbirth. Isaiah 54:1–2:

'Sing, O barren woman, you who never bore a child; burst into song, shout for joy, you who were never in labour; because more are the children of the desolate woman than of her who has a husband', says the Lord. 'Enlarge the place of your tent, stretch your tent curtains wide, do not hold back; lengthen your cords, strengthen your stakes.'

The idea being conveyed here is that of the promise of fruitfulness, the same theme being repeated for men in Isaiah 56:4–5:

For this is what the Lord says: 'To the eunuchs who keep my Sabbaths, who choose what pleases me and hold fast to my covenant – to them I will give within my temple and its walls a memorial and a name better than sons and daughters; I will give them an everlasting name that will not be cut off.'

He promises that their memory will not be forgotten and that they can be fruitful within his economy. This is a message that many single people in our churches today need to hear. I love my 'spiritual children'; I don't know how they compare with natural children, but I have enjoyed them (mostly anyway!) and thank God for the privilege of seeing so many develop into superb Christians.

The single problem

It has not, it seems, occurred to any of those individuals who are so eager to see me married that my marriage status may be of little concern to God, heaven and indeed even to myself. Heaven, we are led to understand from Jesus' words in Matthew 22:30, is managing quite well without the debates and obsessions related to marriage and childbirth. As odd as it may sound to many, it is my conviction that singleness is a part of God's plan for my life – at least for a season, if not indefinitely. I also believe that it is part of God's plan for everybody else's life, since none of us are born married! I am also persuaded, like the apostle Paul, that singleness can be a desirable state (and not simply because of the pressure of persecution, as the argument so often goes).

I would like you to be free from concern. An unmarried man is concerned about the Lord's affairs – how he can please the Lord. But a married man is concerned about the affairs of this world – how he can please his wife – and his interests are divided. An unmarried woman or virgin is concerned about the Lord's affairs; her aim is to be devoted to the Lord in both body and spirit. But a married woman is concerned about the affairs of this world – how she can please her husband. (1 Corinthians 7:32–34)

13

People often view singleness as the option of the self-centred, of those who are simply living to please themselves. This, of course, can be true, but such self-centredness is also an issue to be contended with by those who are married with families. All too often Jesus' words of Matthew 10:37–38 are conveniently overlooked: 'Anyone who loves his father or mother more than me is not worthy of me; anyone who loves his son or daughter more than me is not worthy of me; and anyone who does not take his cross and follow me is not worthy of me.' The 'family' has too often assumed the status of idolatry in our churches, sadly to the detriment of much else that is important. At the same time this largely Western and individualistic vision of the family has remained limited, sterile and lacking in an ability to be inclusive and expansive. Even our black communities are in danger of adopting this model uncritically.

The emphasis of both the words of Jesus from Matthew 10 and the words of Paul from 1 Corinthians 7 is that the desired focus for the Christian is not to be whether or not they are single or married, nor how long either state might last. Neither is it to be self-centred or family-centred. The desired focus for the Christian as suggested by Jesus and Paul is that, whether married or single, we are to be *God*-centred and *God*-focused. The challenge for single people is to make a success of the single life just as the challenge for the married individual is to make a success of married life. The ultimate concern of both, however, must be to serve God in the strength that God gives, in whatever state we are.

This teaching is virtually ignored by the Church today, which is as obsessed with couples as is the rest of the world. Consequently church life revolves around married people, marriage seminars and almost invariably married leaders. I would be significantly better off if I was given a pound for every occasion that some well-meaning church leader or church member tried to match me up with some eligible but totally unsuitable man. The Church may not call single people lepers but it often treats them as though they were unnatural and therefore incapable of serving God in key leadership positions.

None of the above should be taken to imply that I have no

problems, struggles or difficulties in relation to being single. It simply means that I recognize and value the fact that I have an opportunity as a single person to focus on God's purposes in a way that I would be less able to do if I were married. Indeed, in common with all human beings, I certainly have my problems (ask my best friends). I can also confirm that some of these problems are related to my singleness. However, I do not view singleness in and of itself as a problem. In the same way I recognize that married members of the human race may find that some of their problems are related to the fact that they are married, yet many of these have not reached the preposterous conclusion that marriage in and of itself is problematic. Having said this, it should be remembered that the spiralling increase in co-habitation rates in Western society is at least partly due to the belief that marriage as a concept is to be approached with caution (Scase, 1999, pp. 15–19).

According to Home Office figures, the number of single people in the British population has increased dramatically over the last few years and is set to continue to rise. There are now more singles in the overall UK population than ever before – many of whom have never been married.[1] Included in these statistics are those who have been widowed or divorced. In addition, there are those who are legally married but separated from their spouse.

There are now more adults than ever living alone or in flat- and house-shares. The increasing ratings of television series such as 'Ally McBeal' and 'Friends' may well be an indication of just how many people identify with their lifestyles and resonate with the concerns presented. Whereas 10 per cent of people in Britain lived alone in 1995/96 (CRA, 1998, p. 1) the projection for 2010 is that people who live alone will account for 40 per cent of households (Scase, 1999, p. 15). In 1992 the Evangelical Alliance undertook a survey among some of their member churches and they found that 35 per cent of the adults attending these churches were single, 63 per cent of these had never married, while 4 per cent had been separated, 9 per cent divorced and 24 per cent widowed (Singularly Significant Survey, 1992). A recent trip to my local Christian bookshop revealed a significantly larger selection of books on the subject of singleness than I had witnessed on a similar expedition ten years ago. However, the rhetoric and emphasis of the Church continues to be that of marriage and family, while the message of the world continues to be that of the importance of being in a couple, whether married or otherwise (the parallel is often outstanding). It appears that the major, if not the single problem for people such as myself continues to be that of invisibility. There has been reluctance in the Church and society to both recognize and grant validity to single people as human beings with a potential for wholeness *as singles*. This has meant that many single people have felt pressurized into a disposition that views singleness as an unfortunate and hopefully temporary stage in the process to becoming 'happily' married.

However, as a pastor I can testify that there have been those who, in their headlong rush to alter this 'undesirable' state, have made mistakes both in choosing their partners and starting their families, as well as with regard to their timing.[2] These mistakes might otherwise have been avoided if they had felt more able to value their singleness and had been encouraged to engage in a less fraught and pressured consideration of its merits before exchanging it for a long-nurtured dream of 'family life' that soon turned into a nightmare. Perhaps I should add at this point that what I am writing is not merely academic: I have had a number of opportunities to consider the exchange for myself.

In view of all this, I can hardly comprehend the Church's disbelief or surprise at the news that the divorce rate inside its own walls (I do not believe that the Church is a building, by the way) may well parallel the rate beyond its walls.[3] How can we remonstrate with the world when all the time the pressure that the Church exerts upon its own singles is much like the early air-raid sirens whose own message was also very clear: 'Get inside, your life depends on it!'

Bill and Lynne Hybels, pastors of Willow Creek Church in the US, wrote the following in their book for singles:

Your feelings of misery as a single are nothing compared to the misery of being in a bad marriage. The most miserable people in the world are not single people. They are married people who realise that their marriage was a mistake. (Hybels, 1991, p. 93)

As a result of my pastoral work I have had the opportunity to see at first hand just how true the popular proverb on marriage and singleness has become. Marriage, it has been said, is like a cage. Those on the outside are trying to get in while those on the inside are trying to get out! I am not, however, so scarred by cynicism that I believe this to be true for the majority of marriages. I certainly recognize that the pastoral perspective can be skewed simply by the sort of time that it is necessary to invest when trying to mend broken people and broken lives. But neither am I convinced that the much-vaunted public image of marriage as a proverbial 'bed of roses' is in fact the real one. Apart from anything else, the last time that I had a run-in with a rose bush, it also had thorns!

My approach to the issue of the family is largely informed by the fact that I value the institution of marriage and the lives of children far too highly to see them merely as a means to personal fulfilment. The declaration 'I have always wanted children' is not enough to make us suitable parents. I can remember lots of things that I wanted when I was a little younger – I'm still thanking God that he didn't give me half of them.

Synergy in marriage is, I believe, also profoundly important. This is the ability to make the final equation of two people coming together much more than their mere cumulative effect. This results in each individual becoming more than they could have been had they not interacted at all. This principle is not only true for marriage relationships, it is also found in very deep friendships. In the Bible it is expressed in many ways:

As iron sharpens iron, so one man sharpens another. (Proverbs 27:17)

Two are better than one, because they have a good return for their work: if one falls down, his friend can help him up.

But pity the man who falls and has no one to help him up! Also if two lie down together, they will keep warm. But how can one keep warm alone? Though one may be overpowered, two can defend themselves. A cord of three strands is not quickly broken. (Eccelesiastes 4:9–12)

Contrary to popular belief, the latter passage belongs not primarily to the domain of marriage (except perhaps the part about lying down together). Instead it belongs primarily to the domain of friendship and close working relationships. Ideally a marriage relationship should reflect these themes, but they refer to any close friendship and imply that all friendships are to be valued.

In addition, relationships generally fare better when they are based on friendship and mutual respect rather than on whether or not someone is possible marriage material. If we hang around with our heads buried this far in the sand we can hardly expect to avoid either paralysis or accidents!

Social expectations

The power of peer pressure affects us all in many different ways. I recall how I felt when each of my friends began to get married. The pressure to get in with the project became almost unbearable, and there were quite a few times when I wondered if maybe, after all, there was something wrong with me. This fear was invariably reinforced by two or three well-meaning friends who would imply or ask the same question (always uninvited), sometimes adding that maybe my standards were too high anyway. Unfortunately the pressure didn't end when the majority of them were married, but began again when they started having babies. Undoubtedly much of this pressure was internal and was linked to what I thought was being expected of me and perhaps even to what I had come to expect of myself.

The problem is of course that societal expectations and even our own self-expectations are not sufficient to promote a healthy family life. We need more than expectation: we need commitment. The irony is that commitment is not only a requirement for marriage – it is also a requirement for singleness.

18

No one needs a reminder from me of just how sex-crazed our society is. Not only is sex used to sell everything from cars to furniture, the general expectation of our society is that we must either be having sex, planning to have it or have just had it. It is a culture where it is assumed that where there is any cross-gender intimacy there must also be a sexual 'thing' going on. We live in a culture where friendship is so neglected that even intimate same-gender relationships are viewed with suspicion, and the idea of closeness without a sexual element is well . . . odd! For black women, so long identified in terms of their sexuality and productivity, both of which are portrayed as both negative and dangerous, there enters a whole new dimension of unhealthy and unjustifiable societal expectations.

I lament for the days when as a schoolgirl I used to walk down the street with my arm through my girlfriend's arm, giggling about this or that matter or incident. So it was with profound sadness that I overheard the daughter of one of our young mothers saying to her, 'Mum, don't hold my arm when we're walking down the street, I don't want people to think that we're lesbians.' What kind of society do we live in when the display of affection between a mother and daughter can be construed in these terms?

On my last trip to Ghana it was gratifying to see two men walking down the street deep in conversation hand in hand without causing a stir or raising a suspicious eyebrow: I suddenly felt sane again.

Sometimes it seems to me that the Church has imbibed these same values, believing that if a person is not pursuing a relationship or in a relationship with someone of the opposite sex, then there must be something wrong with them.

I remember one particular occasion when a married couple, both pastors and good friends of mine, asked me whether the reason that I had not yet married was due to the fact that I was a child who had witnessed the breakdown of my own parents' marriage. It was then that I realized that they had wasted considerable time and energy deliberating over the question of why I had not yet married (at that time I was in my mid-twenties). I have to confess that I was somewhat frustrated and angry with

19

them and gave them the answer that they wanted to hear. 'Yes,' I said, 'that must be it.' At the same time I knew that this was far from the truth, but had neither the energy nor the inclination to explain myself to them. The idea that I did not find being single abnormal would have been more than they could have coped with. So I held my tongue: I think, in retrospect, for far too long.

Sex and sexuality

I recall a conversation I had a couple of years ago with one of our church neighbours. The guy was not a Christian and he knew that I was the minister of the Baptist Church, so we would often stop to chat when we met on the street. On this particular occasion he was commenting on how I must have lots of boyfriends 'on the go'. My immediate thought was that he'd simply been watching too much of MTV. But since I understood what he was getting at I told him that this was in fact far from the truth. 'Well, what do you do for sex then?' he asked me, and then suggested that he might be able to help me out! So I quickly explained that as a single Christian I was in fact celibate. At this point he looked at me in wonder and astonishment for what at least seemed like a pregnant pause (in other words it was far too long for comfort), then he asked me if I was all right. I responded that I was very happy, very healthy and that I still had my eyesight. Then came the inevitable question: 'Are you . . . you know?' to which I answered, 'No, I'm not . . . you know.' His parting words were 'Well, if you ever need anything.' Need I add that he was unconvinced.

Although not amused by what I perceived to be a racial element in his question, I have to say that I appreciated the man's frankness. It was a refreshing contrast to the many unspoken assumptions and veiled discussions that I had experienced with older Christians who were obviously embarrassed by the subject of sexuality and were not used to having to 'talk it out' with anyone of any age, let alone a younger person.

Sometimes I am asked how I deal with my sexuality as a single person. If your intention is to pursue a path of asexuality and repression, let me break the news to you now. Not only is this virtually impossible unless you make sure that you are so busy that you have neither the time nor the inclination; it is also an unnecessarily negative approach to something that requires as much positive input as possible. A commitment to celibacy is a challenge to channel our sexual energies into the purposes of God. Our sexuality and our feelings then become our gift to God, allowing us to use our passion in God's service. A passage that has done me a great deal of good is 1 Corinthians 6:13 where Paul quotes the accepted wisdom of his day, writing 'Food for the stomach and the stomach for food'. He then adds, 'but God will destroy them both. The body is not meant for sexual immorality, but for the Lord, and the Lord for the body.' Contrary to popular opinion the stomach was not primarily made for food, neither was food made primarily for the stomach. In the same way it can be said that sexuality is not made for sex at any cost, and neither is sex made primarily for sexuality. Instead both sex and sexuality are made for God. So we are not at liberty to indulge in sexual immorality simply because we feel like it. Instead we can make our feelings and even our temptations work for God. So, rather than seeing them as an absolute nuisance or as irresistible urges, we can begin to view them as opportunities for growth. Talk to God about how you feel (it isn't as if he doesn't know already, so you may as well skip the embarrassment!). Make your sexuality and your feelings a gift to God.

Yes, there will be a level of discipline involved, just as there is discipline in getting up and going to work each day (particularly when you'd rather be somewhere else). There is discipline in sustaining good relationships with friends that you value and enjoy greatly; it is no less true in our relationship with God. There is discipline in praying, reading the Bible and meeting with other Christians. There is discipline in fleeing the temptations that will inevitably come (1 Corinthians 6:18). There is also discipline involved in persevering. Anyway, nobody ever said that the Christian life would be easy, just that it would be possible!

Jesus the author and perfector

Jesus, through his words (see Matthew 19:12) and actions, reversed the cultural emphasis on marriage and children. Through his own lifestyle he demonstrated that God not only considers single people to be whole human beings but also that they are able to serve him. Jesus provided a revolutionary role model for believers who may never have seen unmarried religious leaders before.

Jesus, however, is not the only significant single person in the Bible. Old Testament examples include Jeremiah, Elijah and Elisha. The New Testament presents a strong case for viewing the apostle Paul as a single man. In addition there is John the Baptist, Mary Magdalene, Martha, Mary and Lazarus. There is evidence that Luke, the writer of the gospel, was also a single man. Likewise there is Silas, Barnabas, Timothy, Titus, Epaphroditus, Apollos, Lydia, Dorcas, Phoebe and Philip's four unmarried daughters described as prophets in Acts 21:9. These are all presented as single people in the biblical account. In the first century then, it was, ironically, the Church that provided an escape from both societal pressures and cultural pressures to marry and reproduce.

Finally

There are many things that I have left unwritten and many experiences that I have not shared. I have done so mainly because there is a limit to what it is possible to write in a short chapter such as this. I have also spent much time labouring the point regarding the validity of being single in today's world and in today's Church. I need to emphasize that this is not because I do not believe in marriage. On the contrary, I would be quite happy to be married. However, I am also quite happy to be single. I have written in this way largely because my own journey as a single black woman has involved my having to negotiate pitfalls largely created by well-meaning others on so many occasions. Also, I have come to value what God has developed in me through this journey. I have personally sought to hear and obey the still, small voice of the Lord above the cacophony of voices calling out instructions on how it should all really be.

Notes

1 The government Actuary's department projected in 1999 that the proportion of the adult male population who have never married will increase from 32 per cent (1996) to 39 per cent (2011) and from 24 per cent (1996) to 31 per cent (2011) amongst the female population.
2 Many people marry too quickly, without adequate preparation and with little serious consideration for what they are doing and what it may mean in the longer term. Interestingly the US divorce rates were found to be lowest for both men and women who married later in life, at around 28 years of age. Quoted in Albert Y. Hsu (1997) *Singles at the Cross Roads: A Fresh Perspective on Christian Singles*, Illinois: Intervarsity Press, p. 19; from Tom Lasswell and Ntarcia Lasswell (1987) *Marriage and the Family*, California: Wadsworth Publishing, p. 167.
3 It is estimated that 40 per cent of current marriages end in divorce. Although it is recognized that those who share a religious cormmitment are more likely to have stable unions, the rise in divorce rates in among professing Christians mirrors those in society at large. See Jack Dominian (1986) *An Introduction to Marital Problems*, London: Fount Paperbacks.

References

Christian Research Association (1998) 'Information to steer by' in *Quadrant*, London, May.
Hybels, W. and L. (1991) *Fit to be Tied*, Grand Rapids, Michigan: Zondervan.
Mbiti, J. S. (1969) *African Religions and Philosophy*, London: Heinemann.
Scase, R. (1999) *Britain Towards 2010: The Changing Business Environment*, Office of Science and Technology, Economic and Social Research Council.
Singularly Significant Survey (1992) in *Singularly Significant Coalition Publication*, Evangelical Alliance, Issue 3, London.

HERMENEUTICAL INSUBORDINATION TOPPLING WORLDLY KINGDOMS

Mukti Barton

Dr Mukti Barton is Tutor in Black and Asian Theology at Queen's Theological College, and Bishop's Adviser for Black and Asian Ministries in the Anglican Diocese of Birmingham. Born and raised in West Bengal, India, she lived in Bangladesh from 1981 to 1992 where she founded the ecumenical Women's Leadership Training Centre. Her PhD thesis has been published under the title: *Scripture as Empowerment for Liberation and Justice*. Her other publications include *Creation and Fall and the Women of Bangladesh*. Mukti sees her vocation as the empowerment of oppressed people with the help of the scriptures.

God's truth is making people free

In this paper I will concentrate on one aspect of women's life, their role in the Church. It is taken for granted that men play a role in Church life. Whether women have a role, and if so, what kind of a role, is still a debatable question in churches. The debate started about 2,000 years ago at the birth of the Church and is still going on. In some churches, but certainly not in all, women and men assume identical roles. Churches that allocate women a secondary role do so on the basis of the Bible. Therefore I will bring some biblical women out of the shadows to show what roles they played in the time of Jesus and in the early Church. The readers of this chapter are then left to decide what roles women should play in churches today.

As the biblical women's voices are heard and their characters are brought out to light from obscurity, hopefully a glimpse of God's upside-down kingdom will be given. This process will challenge the churches to see whether they are part of God's upside-down kingdom or the world's patriarchal kingdom.

In the last 50 years Christians have achieved what they failed to gain in the previous 1,950 years. Not only on issues of gender, but on other issues such as that of race and class, Christians have begun to ask some very serious questions. These will have to be answered by the churches. In the last 50 years something unique has been happening in Christian history. It seems as if the prophecy of Joel is being fulfilled:

I, the Lord, am your God and there is no other. And my people shall never again be put to shame. Then afterward I will pour out my spirit on all flesh; your sons and your daughters shall prophesy, your old men shall dream dreams, and your young men shall see visions. Even on the male and female slaves, in those days, I will pour out my spirit. (Joel 2:27–29)

The Spirit is poured out on the rich and poor, male and female, young and old, so that God's people 'shall never again be put to shame'. Innocent sufferers are especially God's people, since they suffer just for who they are as created in God's own image. Throughout human history non-white people, especially women, have suffered the most. In the last 50 years women and non-white people are the ones who have risen up in an unprecedented way. They are the authors of the prophetic theologies, the theologies of liberation.

The powerless and the oppressed of the world have learnt how to look at their society, their church and their scripture from the perspective not of the powerful, but of the powerless. As a result they discard their false consciousness, the belief that the colour of their skin or their genitalia make them inferior to the others. They claim God's truth, and the truth makes them free to challenge the injustices of the world.

For Christian women, God's truth comes from their own experience of innocent suffering and from the Bible. The primary source for all church doctrines is the Bible. Yet, according to some doctrines women may be ordained, and according to some others they may not. In some doctrines equal roles are designated to both men and women, while in others only secondary roles are allocated to women. This phenomenon raises the question about how churches which read the same Bible can have such serious discrepancies. The truth is, Christians have read and will always read the Bible differently from each other. They read it from their particular perspective in their own context: there is no other way of reading the Bible or any other books. Therefore, it is natural that different groups of Christians have different doctrines. This is fine, as long as the Bible does not become oppressive to some people. History gives evidence that the Bible has been and is used to oppress various groups of people. In the name of the Bible slavery, racism, colonialism and women's oppression have been sanctioned. Although this has happened, many oppressed Christians are unwilling to blame the Bible itself for their oppression. This is where the whole question of hermeneutics arises. The blame is removed from the Bible and placed where it belongs, on the readers. Gustavo Gutierrez, the father of liberation theology, understands that,

> Human history has been written by a white hand, a male hand, from the dominating social class. The perspective of the defeated in history is different. Attempts have been made to wipe from their minds the memories of their struggles. This is to deprive them of a source of energy, of an historical will to rebellion. (1984, p. xix)

Not only biblical hermeneutics, but all academic disciplines have been affected by the bias of the powerful. In the absence of the voice of the powerless, traditional hermeneutics has often been oppressive to the losers in history. In patriarchal cultures women have been the losers. My argument is, 'If the interpretation of scripture is undertaken only by the powerful in a society, they will consciously, and more frequently unconsciously, continue to legitimise structures of oppression' (Barton, 1999, p. 154). Until recently it was assumed that all biblical interpretation must submit itself to the dominant way of interpreting the Bible. The dominant method was believed to be an objective, value-free and scientific method relevant for all people. The challenge to the traditional method has come from 'the recognition that biblical interpretation is not isolated from the social

26

and cultural values and political interests of the interpreter' (Weems, 1993, p. 216). Class, race and gender affect people's interpretative context for them. When churches read the Bible from exclusively male perspectives, women have secondary roles. When women's perspective is respected, eyes are opened to see God's truth in a new way. The truth makes women free from prejudicial treatments. Equilibrium is established and there is the possibility for all people to use their gifts for God.

The Bible was written by men in patriarchal societies, and therefore in the biblical text itself female voices are hidden or even silenced. Certainly these voices are not as obvious as male voices. Here the interpreters can play a part by further silencing the voices of the biblical women. Renita J. Weems raises a question about the interpreters, 'whose voice the scholar–interpreter "hears", recovers, probes, scrutinizes and interprets within the Bible is also a decision about whose voice is not heard' (Weems, 1993, pp. 219–20). My hermeneutical aim as a woman scholar is to make these silenced voices heard. As the biblical women's voices are heard and their characters are brought out to light from obscurity.

In God's kingdom the humble are lifted up

The patriarchal Church has always taught women to be humble and subordinated to men. As a result, many women now have low opinions of themselves. They have let men have their way at women's own expense. Some women have brought on their own ruin by giving up their rights. The Bible says:

> Don't underrate yourself. Humility deserves honour and respect, but a low opinion of yourself leads you to sin. Do not let others have their way at your expense; do not bring on your own ruin by giving up your rights. (Sirach 4:20–22)

According to the Wisdom of Jesus son of Sirach, these lead you to sin. This book of the Bible goes on to say: 'Stand up for what is right, even if it costs your own life; the Lord God will be fighting on your side' (Sirach 4:28).

27

The biblical good news is not that the humble will be more humbled, but that the humble will be lifted up and the mighty be brought down. Jesus went about putting this good news into practice. God's standard, which Jesus showed, is just the opposite to the standard of the world. The last in the world's standard is first in the eyes of God. Paul, in his letter to the Corinthians, writes:

> But God chose what is foolish in the world to shame the wise; God chose what is weak in the world to shame the strong; God chose what is low and despised in the world, things that are not, to reduce to nothing things that are, so that no one might boast in the presence of God. (1 Corinthians 1:27–29)

God's standard is reflected in the life of Mary, when 'the Word of God', Jesus, came not through a man, but through a woman, Mary. This is why Mary sang out: 'God has brought down the powerful from their thrones, and lifted up the lowly' (Luke 1:52). Mary means 'rebel' and her Magnificat was heralding rebellion (Honculada, 1992, p. 218). Luke records that when baby Jesus was presented in the temple 'There was . . . a prophet, Anna . . . She never left the temple but worshipped there with fasting and prayer night and day. At that moment she came, and began to praise God and to speak about the child to all who were looking for the redemption of Jerusalem' (Luke 2:36–38). Anna, a woman, spoke about Jesus in the temple. The world's standard is reflected in churches when it is taught that women must not preach the word of God.

In his long theological discussion with the Samaritan woman, Jesus, son of a rebel, rebelled against patriarchal customs. He disclosed to her that he was the Messiah. Jesus trusted the Samaritan woman to give testimony to the Samaritans. Her testimony brought the Samaritans to Jesus. She was one of the first missionaries (John 4). Mary of Bethany (another rebel) sat at Jesus' feet listening to Jesus. 'Sitting at somebody's feet' means being a disciple. Together with Mary, Jesus rebelled and taught Mary theology and affirmed her by saying: 'Mary has chosen the better part, which will not be taken away from her' (Luke 10:42). Churches have often taken away from women what Jesus affirmed. Martha also broke down stereotypes. Martha headed and owned a household. 'Mar' is Aramaic for lord or master and 'tha' is its feminine ending (Honculada, 1992, p. 218). Usually church teachings create a division between Martha and Mary, by preaching that Mary chose the better part. However, juxtaposing Luke's and John's versions of Martha–Mary episodes, it becomes clear that Martha was no less a disciple of Jesus. While Mary's voice is hardly heard in the gospels, Martha is vocal. One of the longest intellectual–spiritual dialogues recorded in the gospels is between Jesus and Martha. Martha recognized Jesus as the Messiah: 'Yes, Lord, I believe that you are the Messiah, the Son of God, the one coming into the world' (John 11:27). In order to elevate men, the Church remembered Peter's identical confession: 'You are the Messiah, the Son of the living God' (Matthew 16:16). Martha never received any credit for her confession. The politics of omission in biblical hermeneutics has effectively silenced biblical women like Martha, making women silent in churches.

Jesus' own economic, social, political and religious conditions kept women bent double. In the synagogue, women had no right to enter the areas reserved for male religious leaders. Jesus challenged the oppressive patriarchal system by inviting a bent-double woman to trespass into the male areas. Jesus' healing touch made her stand with her head high. Jesus also challenged exclusive male language by referring to the woman as a 'daughter of Abraham' (Luke 13.16). 'Son of Abraham' was a commonly used term, but 'daughter of Abraham' was unheard of.

According to Mark, a woman anointed Jesus on the head. In ancient Israel, kings were anointed on the head by prophets at the beginning of their reign (1 Samuel 10:1). Christ means 'the anointed one'. It was a woman who performed the task of a prophet and anointed Jesus. Anointing was also a preparation for burial. Jesus' disciple, Judas, involved himself in the plotting to kill him. Peter showed his unwillingness to believe when Jesus spoke about his impending suffering and death (Matthew 16:21–23). The nameless woman in Mark grasped the truth and prepared Jesus for his burial. Appreciating this understanding and support of the woman, Jesus said, 'Truly I tell you, wherever the good news is proclaimed in the whole world, what she has done will be told in remembrance of her' (Mark 14:9). Many churches have suffered amnesia and have not given to this woman the honour that Jesus bestowed on her. Churches have also done a character assassination of her by confusing her with a sinful woman who anointed Jesus' feet. Moreover, for no reason whatsoever the churches have defamed Mary Magdalene by identifying her with the sinful woman. However, the gospels never called Mary Magdalene sinful.[2] Moreover, it is on the testimony of Mary Magdalene and other women that Christianity is standing.

When most, if not all, of the male disciples fled, women walked with Jesus to the cross and remained under the cross. Women were there at his burial and went to anoint Jesus on the Easter morning. For this reason Jesus also honoured women, especially Mary Magdalene, by first appearing to Mary and other women after the resurrection. Jesus sent Mary Magdalene to the apostles with the command 'Go and tell.' Based on the biblical accounts, Mary Magdalene can be called an apostle to the apostles. Neither Jesus, nor the Bible, but the churches silenced women. While the truth of Christianity actually stands upon women's preaching about the resurrection, women are forbidden to preach in some churches.

St Paul sometimes understood the standard of God and sometimes he was influenced by the patriarchal way of thinking. All the gospels give evidence that the risen Christ appeared to women first, but Paul forgot to mention any of the women in his list in 1 Corinthians 15:5–8. He mentioned some men and left the others unnamed. Perhaps it is another sign of male amnesia. Women often mark how patriarchy makes some perfectly saintly men forget about women's gifts and contributions. However, in spite of Paul's weaknesses, credit must be given to Paul for many wonderful sayings such the following: 'There is no longer Jew or Greek, there is no longer slave or free, there is no longer male and female; for all of you are one in Christ Jesus' (Galatians 3:28). All barriers are broken down in Christ. Paul not only spoke about such unity, he and the first Christians worked hard against patriarchy to build up an egalitarian Church.

The early Church clothed women with greater honour

Has the Church progressed or regressed? This is the question to ask when I survey more of the New Testament to present a few biblical women's names in the beginning of Christianity.

'Now in Joppa there was a disciple whose name was Tabitha, which in Greek is Dorcas. She was devoted to good works and acts of charity' (Acts 9:36). Here a woman is clearly identified as a disciple. It is like the tip of an iceberg, indicating that there might have been other women disciples who were not clearly identified as such. There are some verses in the Bible which put women together with Jesus' disciples. 'Soon afterwards he (Jesus) went on through cities and villages, proclaiming and bringing the good news of the kingdom of God. The twelve were with him, as well as some women . . . who provided for them out of their resources' (Luke 8:1–3).

> . . . they went to the room upstairs where they were staying, Peter, and John, and James, and Andrew, Philip and Thomas, Bartholomew and Matthew, James son of Alphaeus, and Simon the Zealot, and Judas son of James. All these were constantly devoting themselves to prayer, together with certain women, including Mary the mother of Jesus, as well as his brothers. (Acts 1:13–14)

These verses give the impression that women were part of the core group of Jesus' disciples. Women have always heard from their churches that it is natural that men have prominent positions in churches, since Jesus only chose male disciples. However, in the patriarchal society of Jesus' time, God's standard is reflected not so much in the ordinary events of Jesus' choice of his male disciples, but in the extraordinary events of women walking together with the male disciples, women who provided for Jesus' group out of their own resources.

A certain woman named Lydia, a worshipper of God, was listening to us; she was from the city of Thyatira and a dealer in purple cloth. The Lord opened her heart to listen eagerly to what was said by Paul. When she and her household were baptized, she urged us, saying, 'If you have judged me to be faithful to the Lord, come and stay at my home.' And she prevailed upon us. (Acts 16:14–15)

Patriarchal standards are turned upside down. Following the lead of a woman, her whole household was baptized. The first churches started in homes like Lydia's.

'There he (Paul) found a Jew named Aquila . . . with his wife Priscilla' (Acts 18:2). In Romans 16:3–4 more is written about this couple. Paul writes, 'Greet Prisca and Aquila, who work with me in Christ Jesus, and who risked their necks for my life, to whom not only I give thanks, but also all the churches of the Gentiles.' Prisca and Aquila, co-workers of Paul, are mentioned six times in the New Testament (Acts 18:1–3, 18, 24–26; Romans 16:3; 1 Corinthians 16:19; 2 Timothy 4:19). Four out of the six times the woman's name is mentioned before the man's. This is still unusual even today. Priscilla and Aquila taught Apollos, a preacher who had thorough knowledge of the scripture. Here again Priscilla's name is mentioned first (Acts 18:24–26). Most probably Priscilla was a better theology teacher than her husband.

Luke writes in Acts 21:8–9 'we went into the house of Philip the evangelist, one of the seven, and stayed with him. He had four unmarried daughters who had the gift of prophecy.'

In Romans 16:7, Paul implores, 'Greet Andronicus and Junia, my relatives who were in prison with me; they are prominent among the apostles, and they were in Christ before I was.' Many scholars now agree that Junia is the name of a woman, a woman apostle (Witherington III, 1988, p. 115).

Romans 16:1 reads, 'I commend to you our sister Phoebe, a deacon of the church at Cenchreae, so that you may welcome her in the Lord as is fitting for the saints, and help her in whatever she may require from you, for she has been a benefactor of many and of myself as well.'

Paul writes to Timothy, 'I am reminded of your sincere faith, a faith that lived first in your grandmother Lois and your mother Eunice and now, I am sure, lives in you' (2 Timothy 1:5). Here Paul remembered to give credit to two women for Timothy's faith and work.

In the first churches women were not just church cleaners and flower arrangers: they are mentioned as disciples, teachers, prophets, apostles and deacons. It seems it was not stipulated that women should remain single to work for the Church, or that they should only work as partner to their husbands. Some of the early church women were single and some were married. Moreover, the married women were not helpmeet to their husbands: they were church workers in their own right.

Hermeneutical insubordination will topple worldly kingdoms

In the kingdom of the world, men rule and women are kept in subordinate positions. If the same happens in the Church, it is clear that the Church is mirroring the kingdom of the world, rather than the kingdom of God.

> For just as the body is one and has many members, and all the members of the body, though many, are one body, so it is with Christ.
> . . . the members of the body that seem to be weaker are indispensable, and those members of the body that we think less honourable we clothe with greater honour, and our less respectable members are treated with greater respect; whereas our more respectable members do not need this. But God has so arranged the body, giving the greater honour to the inferior member, that there may be no dissension within the body, but the members may have the same care for one another. (1 Corinthians 12:12–25)

When women are regarded with less honour in patriarchal societies, in the Church they must be treated with greater respect. Men who have power and authority in the world, will not need it in the Church. Although church leaders often confuse their leadership with worldly leadership, Jesus was clear how his followers should behave:

> But Jesus called them to him and said, 'You know that the rulers of the Gentiles lord it over them, and their great ones are tyrants over them. It will not be so among you; but whoever wishes to be great among you must be your servant, and whoever wishes to be first among you must be your slave; just as the Son of Man came not to be served but to serve, and to give his life a ransom for many.' (Matthew 20:25–28)

If male church leaders understood their ministry to be one of humble service, exercised in a Christlike manner, there would not be any more room to question whether women are called to do the same or not.

Patriarchy and all domination will end when we, the oppressed of the world

> continue to search for something available in this (the biblical) canon(s) – something hidden, something familiar, but something eternal – that will inspire us to fight on and sing a newer song. It is our stubborn faith that even our small, uncelebrated, but persistent acts of hermeneutical insubordination will eventually topple kingdoms. (Weems, 1993, p. 222)

This article is an example of such hermeneutical insubordination and the aim is to topple worldly kingdoms.

Notes

1 All biblical references are from the New Revised Standard Version with Apocrypha. However, the quotes from Wisdom of Jesus son of Sirach are from the Good News Bible with Apocrypha/Deuterocanonical Books.
2 Compare Matthew 26:1–13, Mark 14:1–11, Luke 7:36–48, John 12:1–8; for Mary Magdalene see Luke 8:1–3.

References

Barton, Mukti (1999) *Scripture as Empowerment for Liberation and Justice: The Experience of Christian and Muslim Women in Bangladesh,* Bristol: CCSRG, Dept of Theology & Religious Studies, University of Bristol.

Gutierrez, Gustavo (1984) 'Where hunger is God is not', *Witness,* April 1976, p. 6, cited in Elisabeth Schussler Fiorenza, *In Memory of Her: A Feminist Theological Reconstruction of Christian Origins,* New York: The Crossroad Publishing Company.

Honculada, Jurgette (1992) 'Martha and Mary: the burden and blessing of gender', in Lee Oo Chung *et al.* (eds), *Women of Courage: Asian Women Reading the Bible,* Seoul: Asian Women's Resource Centre for Culture and Theology (AWRC).

Weems, Renita J. (1993) 'Womanist reflections on biblical hermeneutics', in J. H. Cone and G. S. Wilmore, *Black Theology, a Documentary History,* Vol. 2, Maryknoll, New York: Orbis Books.

Witherington III, Ben (1988) *Women in the Earliest Churches,* Cambridge: University Press.

DECONSTRUCTING PATRIARCHY

Dionne Lamont

Dionne Lamont is married to Gee and they have two children, Sean and Lauren. She is currently serving as Assistant Pastor to her local church. Alongside this role, she has served in numerous positions within her church organization and is currently the National Youth Director as well as serving on various committees. Dionne has studied English and Theology and is presently studying Law. She is considered an anointed preacher and teacher of the word of God. Her interests include music, Greek mythology and romantic novels. Dionne also has a passion for card games.

> What are little boys made of?
> What are little boys made of?
>> Frogs and snails and puppy dog tails,
>> that's what little boys are made of.
> What are little girls made of?
> What are little girls made of?
>> Sugar and spice and all things nice,
>> that's what little girls are made of.

This rather quaint, tongue-in-cheek nursery rhyme reflects the old mythical thinking that all things brutish, rough and indelicate are probably male and things soft, tender and genteel are obviously female. 'Boys don't cry' and to do so is to risk being labelled a 'sissy' or a wimp. Girls, however, are expected to cry and dab their eyes with their pretty laced-handkerchiefs held between their dainty little fingers. Historically, the female of the species has always been considered inferior to her male counterpart. The usual argument applies: men are physically able to work manually because of their physique – broad chest, strong arms, etc., and they project an image of strength, albeit physical. A woman's body is built for motherhood, its physique more refined and delicate, primarily to attract its male counterpart by its beauty and to protect any offspring by its reserves in natural energy.

At the risk of stating the obvious, men and women are different (my great moment of enlightenment). The roles of men and women are socially and genetically determined, thus the physical difference predisposes them to different roles and functions.

Traditionally men were always considered superior and women had a more subservient role, 'their place being in the kitchen'. Throughout history we see women fighting for equality. Emmeline Pankhurst established the Women's Social and Political Union. Pankhurst's suffragettes soon won a reputation for boldness and militancy. She dedicated her cause to the rights of women to share on equal terms with men the political privileges afforded by representative government and, more particularly, to vote in elections and referendums and to hold public office. Some thinkers have advocated equal political rights for women since antiquity. Under the autocratic forms of government that prevailed in ancient times and under the feudal regimes of the Middle Ages, however, suffrage was so restricted, even among men, that enfranchisement of women never became a political issue.

Speaking recently with numerous women in ministry, the general consensus is that today in the Church, women, particularly those in ministry, are still faced with a degree of discrimination, dogmatism and narrow-mindedness. These precious women who are in ministry feel that they have to challenge male leadership because, as so many women even in the secular sphere have found, it is 'a man's world'. One of my female colleagues in the ministry said, 'One almost has to forget one's femininity so as to be treated with the same degree of respect as our male ministers.' When I probed her for clarification, she went on to explain that when a woman is assertive she is adjudged to be aggressive, but when a man is aggressive it is considered normal and manly and is interpreted as being assertive. Therefore, women have to don themselves with the 'boardroom' mentality and take the risk of being labelled aggressive or 'a hormonal wreck' and take the bull by the horns in order to make changes.

In researching this subject I have come across various schools of thought; it is therefore not my intention to bring some theological argument as to why women should or should not be ordained to be a deaconess, or bishop, or even an overseer. However, I must admit to finding the reasons for not doing so bizarre, in the sense that those who oppose and claim to be upholders of the scriptures are upholding something which, according to my knowledge, is clearly unscriptural. What I will address, however, is the fact that our interpretation and indeed understanding (and misunderstanding) of scripture, particularly those difficult passages, are often clouded by our culture and social environment.

Jesus Christ did not call any woman to become part of the twelve. If he acted in this way, it was not in order to conform to the customs of his time, for his attitude toward women was quite different from that of his milieu, and he deliberately and courageously broke with it.

For example, to the great astonishment of his own disciples Jesus converses publicly with the Samaritan Woman (cf. Jn 4, 27); he takes no notice of the state of legal impurity of the woman who had suffered from haemorrhages (cf. Mt 9, 20–22); he allows a sinful woman to approach him in the house of Simon the Pharisee (cf. Lk 7, 37ff); and by pardoning the woman taken in adultery, he means to show that one must not be more severe towards the fault of a woman than towards that of a man (cf. Jn 8, 11). He does not hesitate to depart from the Mosaic Law in order to affirm the equality of the rights and duties of men and women with regard to the marriage bond (cf. Mk 10, 2–11; Mt 19, 3–9).

In his itinerant ministry Jesus was accompanied not only by the twelve but also by a group of women: 'Mary, surnamed the Magdalene, from whom seven demons had gone out, Joanna, the wife of Herod's steward Chusa, Susanna and several others who provided for them out of their own resources' (Lk 8, 2–3). Contrary to Jewish mentality, which did not accord great value to the testimony of women as Jewish law attests, it was nevertheless women who were the first to have the privilege of seeing the risen Lord, and it was they who were charged by Jesus to take the first paschal message to the apostles themselves (cf. Mt 28, 7–10; Lk 24, 9–10; Jn 20, 11–18) in order to prepare the latter to become the official witnesses to the resurrection . . . It must be recognised that we have here a number of convergent indications that make all the more remarkable the fact that Jesus did not entrust the apostolic charge to women. (Wijngaards, 1986a)

According to John Wijngaards in his discourse on the Roman document given in *Did Christ Rule Out Women Priests?* (1986b) this argument suggests that Jesus was influenced by the general practice of his time and he portrayed this by selecting an all-male apostolic team. Some commentators argue that if Jesus broke with the social myth of male predominance and yet refused to admit women to the apostolic team, we have a clear indication that he was setting a permanent norm. The Roman document does not prove conclusively that Jesus 'deliberately and courageously' broke with the social attitude of his day. Evidence can be adduced to show that Christ indeed conformed to the social myth of male predominance in several ways. First, the Jews regarded the man as the head of the household, and his family were his possessions (Psalms 128:3). As head, the father had total authority in deciding the future of his children (Genesis 43:1–15; 2 Samuel 13:23–27). The family property could only be inherited by men, with the exception of there being no male heir, in which case a daughter could inherit (Numbers 27:1–11). The father could distribute the family property to his sons without question (Deuteronomy 21:15–17). This was in Old Testament times, but when we look at the New Testament times we see that the juridical position of man being the head had not changed. In the parable of the prodigal son (Luke 15:11–32) we see the father distributing the property to his sons. Moreover, when we examine the parables told by Jesus, we see the family functioning around the man. In Luke 22:11 we see typically the man as owner of the house, the man who builds the house (Matthew 7:24–27), defends his property (Matthew 12:29), and manages the property (Mark 25:14–30).[1]

The Jewish husband

Jewish thinking was that the wife was owned by her husband, and he actually had property rights over her. Even in the decalogue we see the wife listed among the respected possessions (Exodus 20:17). He (the husband) was at liberty to dissolve the marital bond at will. He could even on certain occasions give her away, like the Levite who delivered his wife to the people of Gibeah (Judges 19:1–30). Jesus' referral to marriage takes the male-centred view. In Matthew 22:1–14 he makes reference to a king, but no mention is made of the queen. Notice it is the bridegroom, not the bride who is celebrated. Even the guests are referred to as the friends of the bridegroom. Using this kind of reasoning we can adduce that Jesus accepted the social relationship between the sexes as he found them in his day.

Furthermore, the Jewish notion of male dominance was also supported by their false idea of sexual functions. They contended that the foetus was solely the product of the male sperm rather than a conjunction of male sperm and female ovum. They used 'sperm' and 'off-spring' synonymously (Galatians 3:16), the mother being seen only as the provider of the womb and the father as the carrier of the 'off-spring'. Sociologically, man was placed on a pedestal; consequently these practices were lived out in his religious life. There was no equality between men and women in religion or in the covenant with God. This concept of inequality began at birth. Upon giving birth, the mother was deemed unclean for a period of time. If she bore a son, she was unclean for 40 days; if she bore a daughter, she was unclean for 80 days (Leviticus 12:1–12). The first-born male was celebrated by offering a special sacrifice, a first-born girl did not count, whilst the male child was required to be circumcised on the eighth day so that he would be a partaker of the covenant (Exodus 13:11–16). In contrast, no such initiation or equivalent rite was performed for women. This was tantamount to meaning

40

that God's covenant was concluded literally with the 'sons' of Israel.

A woman was not able to act as a full person, independently, within her religion (Numbers 40:2–17). In the event of her making a vow, it could only be ratified by her father or husband. They were not permitted to present sacrifices and therefore went to the temple for worship on a voluntary basis rather than on an obligatory basis (Exodus 23:17). Similarly, in government, warfare, family life and business management the temple was a place where men ruled. In this religious context we can see that a woman could never be thought of as a priest. The Mosaic Law prohibited women from holding priestly office, restricting the priestly ministry to Aaron and his sons (Leviticus 8:1–36). Whenever priests are mentioned, they are presented as men. Priests were required to marry a virgin, and only men were allowed to eat the sacrifices, although a priest's wife and daughter could eat from his food.

When David and his friends were hungry and no other food was available except the 'holy bread' of the presentation sacrifice, the high priest gave it to them reluctantly, and only after having been assured that they had not touched a woman for some days (1 Samuel 21:4–6). From this school of thought the ministry of a woman at the altar was literally unthinkable.

Ethics and feminist theology

In answer to the dominance of men in the pulpit and in ministry, some feminist theologians have argued that it is just another example of female oppression by men. This form of feminist theology seeks to reveal the oppressive nature of patriarchal theology. It exposes the various methods of how women have experienced oppression and discrimination both in society at large and within the society of the Church. It also speaks of the experiences of hope, love and faith while fighting for liberation and self-worth.

Although women scholars have fulfilled all the standards of academic excellence, only a very few have achieved faculty status or scholarly influence (Gill, 1995, p. 133). Today, feminist theologians no longer seek merely to become incorporated into the androcentric academy and theological institutions. Rather, women scholars have come to realize more and more that all intellectual institutions and academic disciplines need to be refined and transformed if they are to allow women to participate fully as subjects of academic research and theological scholarship. Feminist studies, therefore, seek to engender, in the words of Thomas Kuhn, 'a paradigm shift from the male-centered scholarship that is produced by the patriarchal academy and church to a feminist comprehension of the world, human life, and Christian faith' (Gill, 1995, p. 133).

Just as feminist studies in general have affected all areas of academic inquiry, so feminist theology has worked for the transformation of theology. It seeks to integrate the emancipatory struggles for ending societal and ecclesial patriarchy with religious vision, Christian faith and theological reflection. If theology is 'faith seeking understanding' then feminist theology is best understood as the reflection on Christian faith-experience in the struggle against patriarchal oppression. If theology, as Karl Rahner puts it, has the vocation to engage the whole Church in self-criticism, then feminist theology has the task to engender ecclesial self-criticism, not just of the Church's androcentrism but also of its historical patriarchal structures. Feminist theology thus begins with the experience of women struggling against patriarchal exclusion and for liberation and human dignity. Just as with other liberation theologies, so a critical feminist theology of liberation understands itself as a systematic exploration and 'second order' reflection on this experience. Its methods are therefore critical analysis, constructive exploration, and conceptual transformation. As a critical theology, feminist theology identifies not only the androcentric dynamics and misogynist elements of Christian scriptures, traditions and theologies, but also those structures of the Church that perpetuate patriarchal sexism as well as racism, classism and colonialism in and outside the Church. As a constructive theology, feminist theological studies seek both to recover and reconstruct all those theological symbols and expressions that reflect the liberative faith experiences of the Church as the discipleship community of equals, the experiences of the people of God who are women.

From an egalitarian perspective, there is neither male nor female in Christ. The question is, when proper exegesis and interpretation are applied, do the holy scriptures restrict women from holding ministerial offices that men are not restricted from holding? Are there men-only positions? In a nutshell, I guess I am really asking about the roles which have been considered by society and the Church as being for men only. Are these God-ordained, or are they the result of sin, or culture? Some may argue that they are God-ordained, but I choose to believe that they are as a consequence of sin and cultural influences.

The arguments against women ministering in the same manner as men are based on a few chosen scriptures which, when applied, seemingly cancel out other scriptures. Those who say there should be no restrictions also base their argument on the scriptures, which they feel counteract the other argument. I suspect that both sides argue from a standpoint of experience and emotion rather than interpretation of those difficult scriptures.

Without a shadow of doubt we know that God has called women and anointed them to ministry. Some would say 'Yes, but they should only minister to women', as though women ought to be dismissed to the 'women's quarters'. Looking back historically, many women were called to leadership and the Church prospered as a result of 'God working through them mightily'. However, they too were hindered to a certain degree, very much like some of us today, our full potential not really being truly realized. In cases where they were allowed to excel, the result was prolific. Some of their testimonies are not widely known because most historical writers were men who, because of their theological or cultural conditioning, selected to omit the experiences of these women. Look at the account found in 2 John: 'the elder to the elect lady and her children, whom I love in the truth'. There are some expositors who contend that this elect lady was in fact a church rather than a woman. Never in their imagination would they see the obvious reading to be that a woman was the leader of a 'house church' and the children were those who attended.

Throughout the book of John we see the writer referring to the believers as children, and the elect lady being charged to keep her 'house' (congregation) from heresy and false teachers. Another example is that of Priscilla. Both she and Aquila had a thriving ministry in Ephesus; they were responsible for teaching the brilliant Apollos. Time and space would not afford me to comment on the likes of Thecla who, like Paul, was thrown into prison because of the faith. Basil commented that not only did she cause many to come to Christ, but that she baptized them too. Catherine of Alexandria was a top scholar and philosopher; her campaign to convert the pagan philosophers of her day was so vigorous that Maxentius the emperor had her executed. Let us also mention Marcella, who was alive during 323 to 410 and lived in Rome. Her home was used for Christian prayer and study of the word of God, she was a skilled Hebrew scholar, and research shows that she was asked by Jerome to settle a dispute about a particular Bible passage. Catherine of Siena went into evangelism and ministry from an early age, she was instrumental in nursing the sick during the Black Plague, and won many to Christ. Frances Willard, the founder of the Women's Christian Temperance Union (Mickelsen, 1989, p. 176) was among the first to object to common sexism in the language of preachers. She wrote 'Preachers almost never refer to the women of their audiences, but tell them about "men" and what a "man" is to be.'

No doubt the debate will go on, but a word of caution in interpreting scripture may be appropriate here. We should always be mindful of what the Bible is saying through God's human servants. What was it saying to the first hearers or readers of that message? One should always bear in mind the history and the culture of the time; careful examination of the literary context of the statement should always be given. The adage 'a text without its context is only a pretext' is always worth remembering. We must always be mindful of the chain of thought and the subject being discussed if we are to really begin to 'rightly divide the word of truth'. Furthermore, we should always ask how is the passage to be understood and applied (if it should be applied). The Bible is filled with regulations for people 'where they were', that were not necessarily meant for all people under all circumstances. For example, Leviticus 19:19 clearly states: 'shall not come upon you a garment of cloth made of two kinds of stuff'. I have never read either in the Old or New Testament that that law was ever repealed. Yet most, if not all of us, wear polyester mixed with cotton, wool and silk. Why? Are we being wilful in disobeying the word, or is it that this regulation was not meant to be universal and timeless? I'll leave you to answer that for yourself.

Likewise, in the New Testament we have 'commandments' which most of us ignore; look at 1 Timothy 5 where instructions were given to the Church about how to care for the widows. Look carefully at how the same Church, which bellows and harps on about 1 Timothy 2:12 (restriction of women ministering), seems not to have read the requirements about how to care for the widows in 1 Timothy 5.

The ministry of Christ was, and still is, about a higher order: 'Neither is new wine put into old wineskins; if it is, the skins burst, and the wine is spilled, and the skins are destroyed; but new wine is put into fresh wineskins, and so both are preserved' (Matthew 9:17). The Gospel of Jesus Christ is 'new wine': it has no place in old wineskins. The old wineskins of Judaism, traditionalism or any questionable cultural practices cannot contain the Gospel of Jesus Christ because it is of a higher ideal and of a far more excellent standard. We have been given the power of the Holy Spirit, and he empowers us and enables us to transcend every barrier. Be it racism, sexism, or oppressive church culture, we have been made free: the poor, the rich, the young, the old, the man, the woman; we are all made one in Christ.

Did not Peter quote the prophesy of Joel?

In the last days it shall be, God declares that I will pour out my Spirit upon all flesh, and your sons and your daughters shall prophesy, and your young men shall see visions, and your old men shall dream dreams; yea, and on my menservants and my maidservants in those days I will pour out my Spirit; and they shall prophesy. (Acts 2:17–18)

This beautiful passage from God's word is so rich, that not only did it 'blow' the custom of the Jews 'out of the water', but it also exposes the discriminatory elements which permeate our church culture today. The passage speaks of how the Holy Spirit would come upon all flesh, not just one special group (the Jews), but everyone would be empowered to deliver the message of Christ. It reveals how both men and women would prophesy (bear in mind at this time women took no active part in the synagogue worship). This message transcends ageism, for the young and old would have visions, and dream dreams. This message broke through the barrier of class. Now, the menservants and maidservants would also prophesy. That is one of the beautiful aspects of the Pentecostal experience, it empowered all; it ignores race, gender and class. The invitation of Jesus Christ is for the whole of humanity to follow him. His is a universal message, therefore this invitation can never mean that he requires that his followers become his physical, racial or psychological replicas.

From the beginning of human life God engineered and guaranteed the uniqueness of every individual. Yes, at times we can be elusive and impalpable, but the mark of the divine is evident in every man and woman. 'Without any one's personal choice, for instance, God made each person a member of a given sex, race and culture' (Magesa, 1996). In the understanding of the relationship between human existence and salvation, diversity must therefore be seen theologically as an irreducible fact. Reduce humanity to requirements of physical, psychological or racial identity among humans beings, and you have the perfect rationale for the destruction of one person, race or gender by the different, dominant other.

To force an identity, in the sense of uniformity, is to desecrate the Spirit, the Ruah of God, that Spirit which has taken shape and is inherent in us all. Look at the atrocities of history, occurrences such as the Crusades, the Inquisition, the slave trade, and the Holocaust. Our news today is filled with accounts of ethnic cleansing, the intolerance against minorities, the rampant xenophobia, and the perpetual subjugation and instrumentalization of women everywhere. Upon examination we see that all of these atrocities have at their foundation the quest of sameness among human beings. Obviously, the Christian faith requires us to denounce and utterly reject this kind of action, it is unwarranted by the Gospel of Jesus. 'Uniformity is contrary to the Divine intention for humanity as far as we can gather from the Christian Scripture.' Faith in Jesus demands that we respect and treasure, indeed we ought to be thankful for, the biological and cultural differences and legitimate diversities that God has given to us. Therefore, because they are given us by God, to practise deliberate exclusion and discrimination because of those differences cannot be sustained on Christian and theological grounds. Unfortunately, worldly models often influence church structures and practice, and some church leaders, otherwise personally good and holy, are often not helped to become leaders of the church community. These structures co-opt leaders into behaving rather more like governors or emperors of the people, often to the detriment and oppression of female ministers.

Surely the Christian message is one that is founded on the liberating and redemptive action of Jesus. The Prophet Micah declares: 'He hath showed thee, O man, what is good; and what doth the Lord require of thee, but to do justly, and to love mercy, and to walk humbly with thy God?' (Micah 6:8). Passionate compassion, mercy, understanding, forgiveness, unaffected love; these are the characteristics of a Christology faithful to the kernel of the message of Christ as demonstrated in his life, as well as shown in the most germane Christian message.

It is my belief that the Body of Christ and the ministry of the Church go far beyond masculinity and femininity; they go far beyond gender. We must recognize that the life of the Body of Christ in relation to the ministry of women in the Church has not yet been fully realized or explored. The real Gospel of Jesus Christ is more than a written text. It must not be reduced to just a written text in our theology of ministry, to do so is to rob it of its impact in Christian pedagogy and on values determining Christian living.

I am aware that the call of God is on my life. I have seen many come to the Lord; many have been healed, and both men and women have been delivered through my ministry. If there has been any occasion where I have been discriminated against on the grounds of my gender, I can only say that 'through God' I have always been 'more than a conqueror'. There have been times where I was not permitted to perform certain ministerial functions, but God has always opened 'another door in another room'. The kingdom of God is not to be viewed as a small place, but a place of 'many mansions'.

I certainly do not believe that only men possess the ability of leadership, or the capacity to make decisions and perform important ministerial functions. Man and woman are the true image and likeness of God (Magesa, 1996). The Church is called to be and mirror this communion of the male and female humanity in God. It cannot reject its androgynous character and remain faithful to itself. Male and female must work as a body. This implies the full incorporation of women into the ranks of ministers at all levels of the Church under criteria more faithful to Christ. Then we can say, as Jesus did, 'Go your way, and tell John what things ye have seen and heard: how that the blind see, the lame walk, the lepers are cleansed, the deaf hear, the dead are raised, to the poor the gospel is preached' (Luke 7:22).

Notes

1 Obviously a cultural practice then (which is definitely unacceptable in our culture today). However, if it is a biblical requirement for our lives, should we not be practising this today regardless of what society dictates? Interesting.

References

Gill, Robin (1995) *A Textbook of Christian Ethics*, New Revised Edition, T&T Clarke Ltd.
Hellwig, Monika K. (1992) *What are the Theologians Saying NOW?* Gill and MacMillan.
Hull, Gretchen Gaebelein (1989) *Equal to Serve, Men and Women in the Church and Home*, Scripture Union.
Magesa, Laurenti (1996) *Christology, African Women and Ministry*, Sedos, Ref. AFER, Vol. 38 No. 2, April.

Mickelsen, Alvera (1989), in *Women in Ministry: Four Views*, Bonnidell Clouse and Robert G. Clouse (eds). With contributions from Robert D. Culver, Susan Foh, Walter Liefeld. Downers Grove, Illinois: Intervarsity Press.

Mott, Stephen Charles (1993) *A Christian Perspective on Political Thought,* Oxford University Press.

Publishing Co. Ltd.

Wijngaards, J. (1986a) *Did Christ Conform to Social Myths?*, McCrimmon Publishing Co. Ltd.

Wijngaards, J. (1986b) *Did Christ Rule Out Women Priests?*, McCrimmon Publishing Co. Ltd.

A BLACK WOMAN AND DEACON: A WOMANIST REFLECTION ON PASTORAL MINISTRY

Lorraine Dixon

Lorraine Dixon is an Anglican minister based at St Martin's Church at Chapeltown in Leeds. She is also currently undertaking a part-time MPhil in Theology at the University of Birmingham. The area of research she is pursuing is the unearthing of the history of black contribution in the Church of England in the eighteenth and nineteenth centuries. In her spare time she likes to go to the cinema, play the ocarina and violin, as well as sing.

Introduction

I am a black British woman of African Caribbean heritage, who is a Christian and Church of England (or Anglican) deacon and priest. In sharing my story I hope that it resonates with other women's stories and experiences, particularly those of black women within church institutions that are perceived as white, male, elitist bastions.

Answering the call to be a deacon

I often tell people of my experiences of being ordained as an Anglican deacon on 28 June 1998. The word 'deacon' was not even part of my consciousness or vocabulary, my calling had been to the priesthood. I have been a Church Army Officer[1] for ten years now, but in recent years became aware of a change in my sense of vocation. 'The Spirit lik mi' I frequently reply when people ask me about God's calling on my life at this point. You see, when the Spirit of God says move, you gotta move! Hence, I went forward to have this calling to pastor tested by the Church, and after a period of many months I was recommended for ministerial training. During my time at theological college, I was vaguely aware that I would be ordained deacon prior to priesting (usually a year before), but there seemed to be an understanding within the Anglican Church that this was as 'priest-in-waiting' or apprentice, not as deacon in one's own right. Therefore, on 29 June 1998, I woke up and thought 'I'm a deacon, what do I do now?' Over the next year, by being and doing the work of a deacon, I would begin to get an answer to my own question. It has been an exciting journey of discovery within St Martin's parish in Chapeltown, Leeds, where I work.

The first thing that I had to discover for myself was that being a deacon was more about *being* than *doing*. I reflected on the words from the Anglican ordination service. These are as follows:

Deacons are called to serve the Church of God, and to work with its members in caring for the poor, the needy, the sick, and all who are in trouble. They are to strengthen the faithful, search out the careless and the indifferent, and to preach the word of God . . . (The Liturgical Commission, 1980)

Growing into the role of deacon involved me trying to put these words into some kind of living reality in my life and ministry. In the mix of situations, including baptisms, weddings, funerals, visiting the sick and distressed, involving myself in the community and so on, I found that I began to develop an understanding of the diaconate as reaching out to the lonely, lost and those on the margins. In this context, I saw my work around racial justice issues as central to my role as deacon. This colours my perception of the office, giving it a socio-political edge.

A black woman and deacon: problematizing the notion of servanthood

The traditional understanding of a deacon is that you are called to be a distinctive sign to the Church and world of the Servanthood of Jesus who came into the world as a servant. Jesus said 'I am among you as one who serves' (Luke 22:27, NRSV). His

51

active ministry to the marginalized, the oppressed and the sick underlined the veracity of that statement. When James and John ask about getting a place of honour in the kingdom, much to the chagrin of the other disciples, Jesus calls them and says:

> You know that among the Gentiles those whom they recognize as their rulers lord it over them, and their great ones are tyrants over them. But it is not so among you; but whoever wishes to become great among you must be your servant, and whoever wishes to be first among you must be slave of all. For the Son of Man came not to be served but to serve, and to give his life a ransom for many. (Mark 10:42–45)

Then again, towards the end of his life, Jesus got down on his knees and washed his disciples' feet, getting his hands dirty in service (*diakonia*) to others and compelling us to do likewise. Jesus laid aside his divinity, emptying himself to become fully human, to become one of us. Yet, it could be said that Jesus came from a position of power. He was a male within a patriarchal system and he was often called 'Rabbi', probably emphasizing that he was a member of the religious establishment, albeit a controversial one. To be called to serve as a male within that context was indeed honourable. However, what is servanthood within sexist contexts when as a woman you are expected to serve? What is servanthood also when one's ancestors were forced to be servants and slaves? It is such questions that began to be raised within me as I took up the office of deacon and was thus called by the Church to serve.

The white history of the Church of England is well documented in the discipline of church history and manifested in scholarly books and journals. However, the black history of the Church is virtually unknown. Black people have been present within the Church of England since the eighteenth century. Their first contact with the Church was through enforced baptism as the servants/slaves[2] of their masters. Yet some black people sought baptism as they believed that once they were baptized they should be as free as their 'Christian' brothers and sisters who were their masters and mistresses. Some black people became ministers of the Church. One of the earliest examples is Philip Quaque, born in 1741 on the Cape Coast. He was sent by his father to be educated in England. Quaque was ordained deacon and then priest in 1765 at the Chapel Royal, St James' Palace (Shyllon, 1977, pp. 56–8). The sad history of the Church of England is that its encounter with black people was through slavery and colonialism; as oppressor and oppressed, not as peers. The racism that arose in this period still stalks the Church and shapes its treatment of people of colour.

Womanist theologian Jacquelyn Grant, in her essay 'The Sin of Servanthood: and the Deliverance of Discipleship' states:

> As critical components to Christianity, the notions of 'service' and 'servanthood', when seen against lordship, may be perceived as a necessary dialectical tension, but when viewed in light of human indignities perpetrated against those who have been the 'real servants' of the society, they represent contradictions . . . Non-white people, it is believed by many white people, were created for the primary purpose of providing service for white people. Likewise, in patriarchal societies, the notions of service and servant were often used to describe the role that women played in relation to men and children. (Grant, 1993, pp. 199–200)

Therefore, it seems that the concept of servanthood has to be problematized, particularly in relation to oppressed groups. Becoming a deacon could possibly mean I was now an institutionalized servant and providing a negative model for others to follow. Growing up in the Anglican Church I had witnessed the regulation of black people to areas of service in the Church and their marginalization from positions of authority and power. They were never encouraged or given the resources to exercise influence in the life of the Church except as mute tokens on the occasional committee. Thus, as a deacon, I did not want to collude with the Church's continued racist attitude towards people of colour as 'hewers of wood', as slaves/servants.

Is it possible to redeem the concept of servanthood, especially as it is central to Jesus' understanding of his ministry? Grant draws on the insight of Rosemary Ruether,

> service must not be confused with servitude. In her [Ruether's] view, 'service implies autonomy and power used in behalf of others.' We are called to service. Our conversion is to accept this call by abandoning previous, inaccurate notions of being called to hierarchical and oppressive leadership and power.[3]

Grant continues by emphasizing that in his approach to people, especially those at the bottom of the social hierarchy, Jesus served others by facilitating their empowerment, by making the last first and engaging with the least of his sisters and brothers. He renounces domination and instead expresses a 'new humanity of service'. As Christians we are likewise called to service. However, the Church has operated through the processes of racism, colonialism, sexism, classism and so on, as though some are to be servants of the servants. Yet we are called to be servants like Christ in a community of baptized peers; this emphasizes mutuality and shared power. 'Justice means that some will give up, and some will gain; but all will become disciples; that is, simultaneously, oppressors must give up or lose oppressive power, as oppressed people are empowered for discipleship' (Grant, 1993, p. 216). In the process of discipleship, true community will arise as we serve Christ in one another as equals. As a deacon then, my role is to join with others in the Church to pray and struggle towards this liberative reality.

Black women as pastoral mentors

There are about 10,000 active clergy in the Church of England; of this number about 300 are black or Asian and of this number probably 30 are black or Asian women. We are, frequently, a lone black voice in our parish or other area of ministry. This has implications for me in terms of growing into my role as a deacon. However, I did have mentors; the black women (includ-

ing those within my current parish) who I have seen over the
years engaging in an active and usually unacknowledged
pastoral ministry. African American poet Kelly Ellis writes this:

> I was raised by Chitterling eating
>> vegetarian cooking
> cornbread so good you want to lay down
>> and die baking
> 'Go on baby, get yo' self to a plate'
> Kind of Women.
>
> Some thick haired Angela Davies
>> afro styling
> 'Girl, lay back and let me
>> scratch yo head'
> Sorta Women . . .
>> I was raised by Women. (Ellis, 1995)

From my earliest years, I realized that my care and support had
come from other women, especially my mum and sister.
Although there had been significant men in my life (such as my
dad), as Ellis writes in her poem 'I was raised [and I would add
'cared for'] by women.' Engaging in pastoral care as a black
woman and minister has made me think about the wider issue of
pastoral care as practised and experienced by black women of
the African diaspora in Britain as a way to provide a method of
working. I will focus on women of African origin from the
Caribbean British community/ies. This discussion I believe is
extremely important as the perspectives of black women (and
other minority ethnic women) have, until quite recently, been
ignored or excluded from theological reflection and publications. African American womanist pastors and scholars have
been at the forefront of a change in this situation. It is some of
the insights of such American writers, as well as British ones,
that form the basis of this chapter.

African paradigms of pastoral care

The history of black women and men in Britain has been documented in such sources as Peter Fryer's seminal book *Staying Power* (1984). According to Fryer, this is a history that spans 2,000 years. In her book *Sojourn*, Zhana states, in relation to recent black British history,

> [it] is impossible to talk about the Black presence in the British Isles in isolation. Discussion of our presence here immediately brings up issues of the slave trade and colonization. When writing about the community of Black British women, it is essential to do so in the context of the Black diaspora. Black women in Britain still identify themselves as West Indian, Afro-Caribbean, African or Asian . . . (Zhana, 1988, p. 12)

Therefore, in considering the question of pastoral care and black women of African Caribbean origin in Britain, the ties that bind such women to the diasporal communities cannot be ignored. Such ties have maintained a cultural continuum that stretches back into Africa and into the present. Patterns of care as well as other cultural expressions give testimony to the power of cultural memory of Africans in diaspora.

Emmanuel Lartey, in his essay 'African perspectives on pastoral care', has described how Western pastoral theology has traditionally been the study of the one-to-one counselling situation between pastor (usually male) and parishioner (usually female). Lartey critiques the clinical, privatized and individual nature of this professional relationship. Further, he explores perspectives also expressed by Elaine Graham which highlight the gender and power issues implicit in this context. Lartey goes on to suggest alternative paradigms from the two-thirds world, in this case the African context. He states that pastoral care in this particular context is wholistic, a both/and discipline. It includes both the 'sacred' and 'secular'; the professional and the lay person; a private–personal as well as a social-political input. Here there is a place for the 'individual' as well as the 'community' as both purveyors of and recipients of pastoral care. Methods employed in communication will include the indirect, symbolic, non-verbal as well as the direct, literal and verbal. Pastoral care activities will have preventative as well as relief functions. (Lartey, 1993, p. 5)

In the excerpt above, as well as in the rest of Lartey's essay, he draws attention to the complex nature of pastoral care in Africa. He explains that many people such as healers, diviners and herbalists are engaged in the activity. This means it is a communal action and not just the role of the Christian minister.

Edward Wimberly in 'Pastoral counselling and the black perspective' raises similar issues to Lartey, but from the perspective of black majority churches of the African diaspora in America. Wimberly highlights what he terms the 'corporateness' of pastoral care and counselling in this setting. This is understandable, as the people who make up the vast majority of such churches are of African heritage and so share many of the perspectives that Lartey has outlined. In an analogous manner to Lartey, Wimberly suggests that this propensity toward corporateness within black pastoral care is deeply rooted in African philosophical ideas. Such ideas include a strong sense of unity or harmony of the individual to nature, to the transcendent God, to the spirit world and to the universe. This is manifested by a powerful recognition of community which 'includes as of essence harmonious relations within and between humans and the unseen world of spirits . . . and Mother Earth . . .' (Lartey, 1993, p. 6). Therefore, in seeking to understand the nature of pastoral care in African settings, both on the continent itself as well as within the diaspora, the concept of communality or corporateness is extremely important. Black women have always held (and continue to do so) a central place in this process. This is underlined by Cheryl Townsend Gilkes who says:

Black women figure prominently in the sacred and secular affairs of black communities. Black women's church and community work represents more than mere support for male organizations aimed at social change. Black women . . . participate in the affairs of local, regional, and national black organizations. (Gilkes, 1997, p. 369)

'Mothering' as one model of pastoral care exercised by black women

Although I am not comfortable with Gilkes' 'artificial' categories of sacred and secular, she does emphasize the crucial place black women have played in the support, protection and advocacy on behalf of the black community. This is pastoral care in a broad and inclusive sense. The model which seems to describe the (often informal) type of pastoral care undertaken by black women is that of 'compassionate, loving mother'.[4] Gilkes places these church and community mothers in a lineage that stretches back to Africa. She provides African paradigms such as 'elder' and West African women arranging themselves into social organizations, to provide a context for understanding why women, especially 'mothers', have remained important to the function of black communities in diaspora. However, the use of 'mother' in the context of pastoral care could be said to relate to many women from the diverse cultures and ethnic groups of Britain. Still, both Austin's and Gilkes' use of 'mother' as model of carer in the black communities is significant. This is because it has been and often still is mainly women, especially mothers, who operate as carers and nurturers. In many black churches this is acknowledged. 'Women are designated "mothers of the church", an honorific title usually reserved for . . . the oldest and most respected members' (Austin, 1995, p. 211). In the introduction to *When Our Ship Comes In*, Palorine Williams explores the role of such mothers in the black communities. She states that:

the daily resistance of Black women against the many insidious ways oppression threatens our humanity goes unseen . . . [They] are the psychological and emotional pillar of the Black communities. The daily onslaught on our people is tempered by the unacknowledged work of women. When young men are beaten up [by racist thugs], they return home to mothers, wives, sisters and girlfriends who lovingly care for them. When homes are smashed up it is the women who painstakingly and lovingly rebuild them. (CBWWG, 1992, p. 5)

In the stories that this group of Leeds-based African Caribbean elder women relate, many themes that could be described as pastoral are explored. Common themes that recur in the different stories are concerns for the spiritual, emotional and physical well-being of young people in a context of racism. These 'mothers' speak of giving not only their own families but also other people from their community 'good advice in love' (CBWWG, 1992, p. 5). Such advice enables the young, especially, to not only 'survive' racism and other oppressions but to develop strategies that enable one to work towards self-determination. The community is seen as being at the heart of the ongoing struggle for healing in the black communities. One of these African Caribbean women elders of Leeds, Joyce Bernard, feels that the unity shown between people is as important as counselling agencies and other organizations. She cites as her example the way that black communities pull together when a family suffers a bereavement. Help and support are given as the family goes through the grieving process as well as the preparations for the funeral itself. Sister Bernard believes that when there is a lack of harmony, a non-'deep rooted "come together"' (CBWWG, 1992, p. 51) within the community, individual black people will not survive the ravages of oppression.

The stories from the book *When Our Ship Comes In*, bear out the truth of Sister Bernard's sentiments on community. The women's recollections include memories of arriving in Britain from the Caribbean and being met by discrimination and 'colour bars'. They, as so many other black women, found ways to work around and against racism. They did this by encouraging their community to work together, to unite in a common goal of empowerment. Their stories are echoed in the book *The Heart of the Race* (Bryan, Dadzie and Scafe, 1985). In Chapter 4 of the book, the ways that African Caribbean women found to organize and sustain their communities are outlined. They established hair salons to cater for black women's hair, but they also provided a safe meeting place to share information and news. Unable to obtain a mortgage or a loan from banks, it was women in the main who established 'pardner schemes'. In these schemes, people could pool their money and withdraw it on a rota basis to put the deposit down on a house or send for children left with family in the Caribbean. Black women too played a major part in establishing churches in their homes and elsewhere, when the Anglican, Methodist, Roman Catholic and other Churches did not welcome them. Others remained in these Churches providing a witness and resistance to racism. These women continue to be the heart of the black communities and provide the focus for the spiritual and political liberation of black people. In the lives and efforts of these 'mothers', the focus of pastoral care is broadened to include not just the minister but also the community. In this role, they seek to meet the 'spiritual, emotional and physical needs of all people, no matter where and how encountered' (Austin, 1995, p. 209).

These 'mothers' are not only the heart of the black communities but its soul. Although commitment to community is important to them, it is a pastoral care that is fed by their love of God and the working of the Spirit. For many African Caribbean women their spiritual lives are focused in the church or on the margins of the church. Indeed, in the black majority churches they are the veritable backbone of that movement. Whilst the pulpit in many (but not all by any means) of these churches may be closed to women, they have located themselves in alternative positions of leadership and pastoring.[5] Their black 'sisters' in the white majority churches, many (but not all) with an open pulpit, are nevertheless marginalized and do not share the same sort of influence. Still, they remain and are nourished in some deep way in their daily lives and ministry by these church traditions.

The Christian faith has, for a large number of black women of the African diaspora, provided a vehicle for their spirituality with its dual dynamic of survivalism and liberation. I remember growing up in a household where my mother would quote scripture or sing spirituals or gospel hymns. I also remember growing up in a black majority church, where the 'mothers' there enabled me to grow in the faith I had been baptized into. They possessed a deep faith that spoke of being somebody in the presence of God: a faith that said that I too was created in the image of God and thus equal to everybody, despite how I was treated as a black person in the wider society.

In this discriminatory society, these women could only find employment in low-paid and unrewarding jobs in factories or as nursing auxiliaries with few prospects. Yet in church, they spoke with power as they testified of their love of God and what he had done for them. In this church the women were not treated like dirt but had their personhood validated. It was their understanding of Jesus as co-sufferer (a term I have borrowed from African American womanist theologian Jacquelyn Grant) that helped me in my struggles as a teenager. I came to have faith in Jesus who inhabits our troubles with us; who we can call on by name when we are at our lowest. This Jesus who helps us survive oppression and shares our burden when it is too heavy. This Jesus who also gives us strength and the hope in our struggles for life free of prejudice, life in its fullest. It was in the faith, hope and the humanity of these women that Jesus came to life in my soul. I was enlivened by the same Spirit that blew through the 'pain and sorrow' places in my life.

The use of 'mother' as a model of pastoral care practised by black women is not without its difficulties. There are people who have not enjoyed a long-term or stable loving relationship with their mother; like the African American spiritual says, they are motherless children. They may have lost a mother to death or divorce. For others, their mothers are very much in their lives but they let them down by neglect, harsh criticism, abuse or by not protecting them from abusers.[6] The concept of 'motherhood' may also be problematic for those who do not have children, for whatever reason. Moreover, Theresa E. Snorton, utilizing the insights of Patricia Hill Collins, warns against the use of limiting stereotypic representations 'to describe black women and . . . justify racist, sexist, and classist attitudes toward them. [Collins] lists four such images: the mammy, the matriarch, the welfare mother, and the Jezebel' (Snorton, 1996, p. 52). Yet these categorizations represent dysfunctional perspectives of motherhood, imposed from outside black communities, that lack depth and warmth. It is important that black women set the parameters of our own self-identity in its widest sense.

However, even bearing in mind these real issues of concern, I still find the idea of mother as a model of pastoral care in the black community a useful one. This is because I have had the privilege of growing up and being cared for by good 'mothers' and not all of them had children or were part of my family. In their lives they made spiritual virtues come alive – values such as commitment to others, generosity and a passionate spirituality which informed their sense of justice. They also spoke truth in a firm but gentle way, furnishing me with boundaries and enabling me to establish a framework for my life; they were mentors. Therefore, as a black woman minister, I wish to use such black women as role models. In them, I have gained a picture of the hospitality and kindness that is a gift from God and says something of the nature of God.

Concluding thoughts

Becoming a deacon has involved me in a hard spiritual journey in some ways. I have felt called to enter a wilderness, and yet there is milk and honey within that desert. In these past few months, I have been led to leave behind old and comfortable ideas about God and appreciate God as mystery. Questions about the suffering of parishioners, as well as big world events, became uppermost in this journey. Part of the journey has involved working out what being an ordained minister actually means. Being in the parish has made me even more aware that we exercise ministry in the context of community and not for our own sake. This has not been an apprentice year in the usual sense of the concept, but one of discovery and growth. It has been a hard but paradoxically a joyful time. It seems to me that attempting to follow in the nurturing and caring footsteps of the women

I have been discussing, serves as an example of how a young minister like myself could begin to engage in an effective diaconal ministry, i.e. serving Christ within myself and in other people. It also acts as a reminder that as a deacon and priest, I do not walk alone but share the work of 'mothering', pastoring with other people, especially these 'mothers' of the black community.

Notes

1 The Church Army is a lay society of evangelists that has existed within the Church of England since 1882. It was founded by Prebendary Wilson Carlile, who was soon joined by his sister, Marie Carlile, who started a women's section.

2 For black people there did not appear to be a difference in status between slave or servant. They were perceived as free or very cheap labour and were unpaid, unlike white servants. See F. Shyllon (1977) *Black People in Britain 1555–1833*, London: The Institute of Race Relations and Oxford University Press.

3 J. Grant (1993) 'The sin of servanthood: and the deliverance of discipleship', p. 203. Grant quotes from Rosemary Ruether, 'Christology and Feminism: can a male savior help women', *An Occasional Paper of The Board of Higher Education and Ministry of the United Methodist Church*, I (25 December 1976).

4 D. A. Austin (1995) 'In the middle of everyday life: the spaces Black clergywomen create', *The Journal of the Interdenominational Theological Center (JITC)*, Vol. 22 No. 2, p. 209. Austin also indicates another model of pastoral care – that of 'midwife'. However, she does not explore this model. Perhaps it is linked to the midwives in Exodus chapter 1 (the Exodus narratives have always played a key part of black religious thought), who, rather than collude with their oppressors, became a focus of liberation. Their actions came out of their love for God and people. This is not unlike the 'mothers' described in this essay, who work for the good of their communities as well as their families.

5 Austin (1995, p. 211) lists the various ministries that women in the black churches are often engaged in. These include 'evangelists, missionaries, stewardesses, deaconesses, lay readers . . . Sunday School teachers, musicians, choir members and directors, ushers, nurses . . . caterers and hostesses for church dinners, secretaries and clerks, counsellors, recreation leaders, and directors of vacation Bible schools.'

6 See bell hooks (1993) *Sisters of the Yam: Black Women and Self-Recovery* (London, Turnaround). In the second chapter of her book, hooks explores the issue of harsh criticism that can occur in black communities, especially in the context of mother and daughter relationships.

References

Austin, D. A. (1995) 'In the middle of everyday life: the spaces black clergywomen create', *The Journal of the Interdenominational Theological Center (JITC)*, Vol. 22 No. 2.

Bryan, B., Dadzie, S. and Scafe, S. (1985) *The Heart of the Race: Black Women's Lives in Britain*, London, Virago Press.

Chapeltown Black Women Writers' Group (CBWWG) (1992) *When Our Ship Comes In: Black Women Talk*, Yorkshire Art Circus.

Chireau, Y. (1995) 'Hidden traditions: black religion, magic, and alternative spiritual beliefs in womanist perspective', *JITC*, Vol. 22 No. 2.

Cobham, R. and Collins, M. (eds.) (1987) *Watchers & Seekers: Creative Writing by Black Women in Britain*, London, Women's Press.

Ellis, K. N. (1995) 'Raised by Women', in C. W. Sherman (ed.), *Sisterfire: Black Womanist Fiction and Poetry*, London: The Women's Press Ltd.

Fryer, P. (1984) *Staying Power: The History of Black People in Britain*, London, Pluto Press.

Gilkes, C. T. (1997) 'The roles of church and community mothers: ambivalent American sexism or fragmented African familyhood?', in T. E. Fulop and A. J. Raboteau (eds.), *African–American Religion: Interpretive Essays in History and Culture*, London: Routledge.

Graham, E. and Halsey, M. (eds.) (1993) *Life Cycles: Women and Pastoral Care*, London: SPCK.

Grant, J. (1993) 'The sin of servanthood: and the deliverance of discipleship', in E. Townes (ed.) *A Troubling in my Soul: Womanist Perspectives on Evil and Suffering*, New York: Orbis.

hooks, bell (1993) *Sisters of the Yam: Black Women and Self-recovery*, London: Turnaround.

Hopkins, D. N. (1993) *Shoes that Fit our Feet: Sources for a Constructive Black Theology*, Orbis Books.

Lartey, E. (1993) 'African perspectives on pastoral theology: a contribution to the quest for more encompassing models of pastoral care', *Contact*, 112.

The Liturgical Commission (1980) *The Alternative Service Book 1980*, London: The Central Board of Finance of the Church of England.

Shyllon, F. (1977) *Black People in Britain 1555–1833*, London: The Institute of Race Relations and Oxford University Press.

Snorton, T. E. (1996) 'The legacy of the African–American matriarch: new perspectives for pastoral care', in J. S. Moessner (ed.) *Through the Eyes of Women: Insights for Pastoral Care*, Minneapolis: Fortress.

Wade-Gayles, G. (1995) *My Soul is a Witness: African–American Women's Spirituality*, Boston: Beacon Press.

Wimberly, E. P. (1989) 'Pastoral counselling and the black perspective', in G. S. Wilmore (ed.) *African American Religious Studies: An Interdisciplinary Anthology*, Durham and London: Duke University Press.

Zhana (ed.) (1988) *Sojourn: An Anthology of Prose and Poetry Reflecting Black Women in Britain Today*, London: Methuen.

THE PROFESSIONAL WOMAN

Angela Sarkis

Angela Sarkis was born in Jamaica and grew up in Nottingham where she attended the New Testament Church of God. She now lives in Harrow, Middlesex with her husband Edward and children Matthew and Laura. Angela is Chief Executive of the Church Urban Fund. Prior to her appointment in 1996, she was Director of DIVERT Trust, a national grant-giving and consultancy agency with the objective of helping local communities develop projects for young people at risk of offending. Angela has many years' experience in the Probation Service in Leeds, Nottingham and Middlesex. She has spent the last decade working in the voluntary sector, is committed to equal opportunities and issues affecting disadvantaged communities, and has wide experience of voluntary organizations both as trustee and staff member. Angela is currently a trustee of BBC Children in Need, a committee member of the Joseph Rowntree Foundation and council member of the Howard League for Penal Reform and the African and Caribbean Evangelical Alliance. Since January 1998, Angela has been a part-time adviser to the government's Social Exclusion Unit.

I am a professional woman. It feels good but it hasn't always been that way. My mother is not a professional woman. She is one of life's unsung heroes – an experienced seamstress who arrived in this country from Jamaica in the mid-1950s in search of a new life. In reality, there were no opportunities for her skills and she worked in a sewing factory to make ends meet while bringing up our family. Rumour has it that she was the fastest 'pieceworker' in her department and, having attained the highest daily rate for the work, assisted friends to do likewise.

My best friend is also not a professional woman – she's a housewife who takes part-time work as a secretary, pastor of a Pentecostal church near me and works in the kitchens of a local school. Mary, who lives two doors down from me, is a professional working in a bank – she rushes home every evening to cook, clean and look after her children.

This, I believe, is the context for many black professional women in Britain. It is certainly the context within which I live and work.

Let's look at the alternative.

My husband is a professional, a solicitor. His father was also a professional. Many of his friends have jobs which could be described as professional. Their career structures are unruffled by childbirth. They see their primary responsibility towards the family as financial, and are often found in pubs and wine bars in the evening, in work-related socializing.

It may not be a better life, but from where I sit it does look easier. Some men wrap their professionalism round them. Like an Armani suit or a Hilfiger top, this one label constitutes a large part of their identity. This is not to say that some men are shallow – far from it, many suffer and are blessed equally by an intense capacity to focus on one thing at a time.

By contrast, many women live with labels from all parts of life – professional, yes, but also wife, mother, auntie, carer, friend, lover. We are not one label, even if we wanted to be. My children would never forgive me if I put them second to anything. But does my work suffer as a result? No.

Professionally, I have been lucky through hard work. That's part of my background, a legacy from my parents. I started out as a probation officer, I was instrumental in founding a charity called DIVERT trying to provide constructive activities for dis-advantaged youths and reducing their likelihood of offending. I was headhunted for the Chief Executive's post at the Church Urban Fund and seconded to the government's Social Exclu-sion Unit. I was made CBE in the Millennium New Year's Honours list.

At the same time, I have two children. I go to the gym when I can find the time. I visit the hairdressers every two months – which I know will shock some of my sisters who have season tickets – and I aspire to be an active member of my local church.

My life has often been a roller-coaster, but I have grown in faith during my career and I have been tested emotionally and physically. I still don't know what to do with prejudice, although I know how to stand against it. I cry just the same over back–biting. I don't know where I stand on the stockings-versus-tights issue. My children are teenagers and have their own heartbreaks for me to think about.

Black women have even more labels and roles to juggle – our culture, faith and gender are particularly sensitive issues. As a Jamaican woman, I know that women in the African Caribbean community are at the forefront of everything, at home, at church and in the community.

Our men can feel threatened by this, especially today as some perceive their role as breadwinner and leader being diminished. A paradox is that, as we challenge and surmount racial prejudice and discrimination and begin to make our mark in Britain, it is our women who are more likely to be successful than men. We are less threatening to white professional society, are more willing to work our way up from the bottom and to combine our ambitions with traditional expectations of mother, carer, cheerleader and chief bottle washer. Some men are discouraged more easily, become more frustrated by blatant inequalities, are less able to be flexible, and they suffer by comparison.

Perhaps as a result of this, some black men feel threatened by black professional women and as a consequence we are increasingly likely to be single. This in itself is a cultural thing. A black woman without children may feel a sense of loss. A black woman without a husband . . . well, many of us have become used to them not being there. Furthermore, women who can only commit themselves to 'born again' Christians and feel unable to cross the racial divide are finding it increasingly difficult to find life partners within our own communities.

You might say that professional women labour under a big disadvantage, with these labels and dilemmas hanging round their necks. It is certainly true that reconciling all the demands made on my time can cause me heartache (and tired feet!). I remember once, when I was still at DIVERT, spending the morning addressing a meeting in the House of Lords. The chairman asked me to stay for the afternoon session. I was flattered, but had a prior engagement which took precedence. And what was the prior engagement? I was booked in to run a race at my daughter's primary school. Did it affect my career? No. Did

I win the race? No – the pressures of my life may have created a versatile person, able to operate at all levels. They have not yet given me Merlene Ottey's legs.

Joking apart, it is precisely because many women have rounded, versatile personalities that they have so much to offer the professional world. This is our unique contribution to the marketplace, and it is what makes us equal partners with men.

At the same time, people are unwilling to believe this. Ignorance about women at work may be less obvious nowadays, but it is just as insidious and, damagingly, more sophisticated. People try to compartmentalize a woman's life, saying that family must take precedence, or that the career is paramount, and that you cannot expect to have it all. At my interview for my first job I was asked about my plans for marriage and raising a family. Ten years later, I was asked in another job interview how my husband would cope with my new responsibilities and priorities.

Life, however, is rarely straightforward and hard choices need to be made. Let me give you two examples.

Once, I was just leaving work to collect my two-year-old daughter from nursery when I heard that one of my clients and her baby had been detained at Heathrow Airport for possession of cannabis. After an unsuccessful attempt to secure the mother's release on bail, I had to choose between arriving on time to collect my daughter and finding a care placement for my client's child overnight. I arrived at the nursery 30 minutes late to find an irritated assistant but a relaxed child.

The second example did not present any such dilemmas. My registered childminder telephoned me at work, clearly under the influence of drink, to inform me what a good job she had made of cutting my twelve-month-old son's hair. Suddenly, my negotiations with the housing department about a homeless family paled into insignificance. The next fortnight was spent on unpaid leave while my mother made arrangements to spend the next two years making the weekly trek between Nottingham and London to care for him.

No, I don't expect to have it all, but I deserve the opportunity to make choices and to be respected for them. What we need as women is a mentor to help us see the way through this and keep our perspective. It is one thing for me to say now that children, husband and faith contribute to my working life. It was quite another when I was trying to work out how they fitted together. Then, there were very few professional women and an infinitesimal number of black professional role models.

My most effective mentor has been my sister. She is a scientist with a clear, analytical mind. She sees through my imaginary veils and has the knack of going straight for the jugular when I need sorting out. As for me, I am a mentor now to many young (and not-so-young) black and white women, rising through the ranks and making a difference to the world. A friend of mine has a whole series of mentors, one for each day of the week.

To tell the truth, I have become wary of taking on any more mentoring commitments. Enjoyable and fulfilling as this form of friendship is, it can also be demanding, both timewise and emotionally. This is because a mentoring relationship goes both ways. There isn't really a question of 'mentor' and 'mentee'. I may be able to offer workwise hints, but I wouldn't derive any enjoyment from the situation if I wasn't also getting feedback on how to cope with gender inequality in the workplace, balancing tensions and priorities, and sharing the frustrations of racism and prejudice that can still make life so hard.

As I say, I am entering into fewer mentoring partnerships, but here are some of the things I say when I do make that commitment.

First, get yourself a career plan. Where do you want to be in five years' time? It is a serious question, and even if your answer is 'Haven't a clue', examine your reasons for that answer. Are you afraid to own up to your ambition and enthusiasms? I know that I was. For many years, if asked, I used to say, 'Oh, I'm not ambitious.' But that doesn't work. If you think about where you are now in relation to so many other people, you're going to sound like a hypocrite saying that.

If you want to be in politics, or at the head of a charity, or running a business, admit it to yourself. Think about it – you're not afraid to admit that you want children or a nice home, are you? And you know how to go about getting those and when you intend to do it, don't you? Well, building yourself a career plan is the other side of the jigsaw. One complements the other.

The basis of this career plan should be practical. Think first about whether your current employment is fully realizing your potential. Look at whether it is preparing you adequately for your next career move. If neither of these is the case, examine what motivates you in the job – it is probably social, family or work factors that have nothing to do with getting you where you want to be.

I'll give you an example from my own life. When we met, my husband and I were both probation students. This gave rise to successful careers in the probation service. It was good work, but we both knew we would eventually want to move on. For my husband, the motivation was to be in a position where he could make more of a difference to the people we helped stay out of prison – he wanted to be a solicitor.

That was his career plan and it was a good one. He wanted to help improve the quality of legal representation for the disadvantaged. He would be intellectually tested in a new area of work. On a family level, we would, when he qualified, have an increased combined salary and all the opportunities that would bring to our children.

There was just one flaw, but I didn't see it until too late. I knew already that I would have to support him during his four years of training, but I hadn't thought it was a problem. What I didn't see was that this would completely interfere with the development of my own career.

For four years, my life was on hold. Fine, I had a good job and I was supporting my family, but I was standing still. I felt I had no choice, that I had to support my family financially, but also that I had to look after my children, do the housework *and* help my husband with his homework. I am sure he enjoyed the attention, but I certainly didn't need to do it. Perhaps he felt a little claustrophobic because of it. I didn't ask. At least there was a light at the end of the tunnel: he would eventually qualify and we would be a two-income household again.

That's an example of what I mean when I say that my job motivation at that time had nothing to do with any career plan:

I was just trying to hold all our lives together. Once I recognized that (and once my husband qualified as a solicitor), it was easier to pull myself together and move on.

The second bit of advice I hand out in mentoring relationships is that you must learn the art of saying 'No', if you are to achieve your full professional potential. As a woman, you will almost certainly find yourself trailblazing at some point, doing something that few women have done before. It is a heady feeling, and one I remember well from my first days as Chief Executive of the Church Urban Fund. I don't think I would have achieved such a fulsome write-up in *The Guardian* following my appointment if it hadn't been for the rarity factor and the fact that my elevation was taking place at the heart of the Church of England.

The trouble is, it is so easy to become carried away with your own achievements. Someone will invite you to be on a committee, or to write an article, or to advise them, or review their staff, or whatever. And suddenly you're tearing your hair out with too much to do. You have created a rod for your own back.

Your core job must be the focus of your professional life. Take on extras only if they directly relate to your career plan – contacts, training or experience. I have a friend who always volunteers for assignments. Sounds daft, I know, but it brings her within closer proximity to her boss so that he can see first-hand the quality of her work.

Anything that doesn't have a direct impact on your career must go. I find this the hardest piece of advice to follow.

Of course, you must be careful to accumulate enough extra-curricular experience to appeal to the working world. This does entail some sacrifice of time. How much you can take on will depend on your capabilities and interests as an individual. The basic rule, however, remains the same: don't set yourself up to fail. Say 'No' if you know you are already busy enough. Each year I begin by assuming I will decline all invitations to speak, or some other activity, unless a strong case can be made for me to say 'Yes'. By the year-end I am disappointed that so many persuasive arguments were made.

The third point is to ensure that your professional relationships help you to remain targeted and effective. I want to mentor people who will supplement my own experience. I want to learn as much as you do, to hear the good news and the bad news that will help me in my own experience. I want to know how you are balancing aspects of your own lives. I don't have the answers – you are probably better organized and more focused than you think. If we have a professional relationship, it must be positive for both of us.

The fourth bit of advice is to keep a balance. If you don't recognize what you lose, along with what you gain, you can lose everything. We've all heard people say that gaining recognition loses you privacy. But it is nonetheless true. Look at what I said about not entering any more mentoring partnerships – a lot of people know about me and want my time. That may be wonderful, but it can also preclude other opportunities.

Read the signposts, even if they are hidden. Your partner, if you have one, will feel vulnerable, either because you are more successful than they or, perversely, because you are paranoid about hurting them and so ruin the respect within your relationship by treading too carefully around them.

Remember that men are both robust and vulnerable. Any man can survive having more money. No man likes to feel that his woman doesn't respect him. He may not have even thought about your salary . . . until you ask him whether it bothers him.

To your partner, you are not a label or a professional success story, neither are you a role model. He may be proud of you and your public persona, but he is the one person to whom you most completely reveal your private self. If your public image intrudes on this too much, he will be offended – and rightly, because you are effectively closing him out.

The same goes for your friends. There is no doubt that, in achievements, you may leave some of them behind. But as long as your private self is not covered over too much by your public image, they won't care. They will think that you are lucky and they may be envious in the abstract, but they won't accuse you of selling out.

Most of my friends, as I said at the start, are not professional, but we have something in common that transcends our everyday lives, called friendship. These enduring friendships began when I was seven or eight. This is what I mean by keeping a balance: you may feel that talking about children or holidays, clothes or film stars is below you, but it is not. You still dress, you still relax and you still lust after the unattainable (occasionally). You are not above this, just because you are good at sitting at a desk and because people look up to you and take you as a role model.

In the same way, you are not above putting on your make-up and going to the gym. I don't know what it is, but as soon as a woman goes through the professional glass ceiling, she ceases to care about her appearance so much. Perhaps the glass ceiling acts as a mirror; perhaps she thinks that male desire has ceased to be relevant to her career.

Whatever the reason, you have to maintain your femininity by outward signs, and that means taking care of yourself. This is not for the outer world, whatever statement you may think you are making. This is to ensure that you retain your confidence in yourself as a physical person. Professions are about brainwork, and it is easy to keep developing this if you take a responsible attitude to professional journals and new developments. It is equally easy to let yourself go physically.

Of course, one subtext to this is that your gender remains an important weapon in your armoury. The sad fact is that, as a woman aiming for the top of your profession, you are likely to be a rarity, although thankfully not unique. If you are black as well, you have added shock value. You can use both these things to get your point across. People may be reluctant to challenge you, and this is a mixed blessing.

That is the secular aspect of my advice to my mentor partners. More important is what, for lack of a better term, is the spiritual aspect. Spirituality and professionalism don't mix, right? People often ask me why I don't burn out. I do work incredibly hard and I am sometimes guilty of ignoring my own precept about keeping a balance, but one thing supports me above all, and that is my faith in God. My passion for work is fuelled by that faith. From the early days of my career, I have struggled to link my faith with what I saw in my childhood: people broken by poverty, ignored by society and still loved by God. I didn't want a faith without works, I wanted an active faith that would enable me to make sense of the reality I saw around me and my experience of a loving and caring God.

As Christians we are sometimes exclusive in our outlook. We fear the unknown and this inhibits our effort to engage with those who live beyond our church doors. This ignorance of the real world means that some of us do not relate our faith to our work lives and miss opportunities to put our faith in action. For me, an active faith challenges the injustices we see around us and brings hope to those who are burdened by it.

I became a probation officer because I felt that it was important not to work only with successful people or those of common faith. Everything I have done in my working life has had this spiritual dimension to it. After all, you cannot see the pattern of your work until you stand back. Faith is the imperative to stand back, survey what you do and make an objective decision that takes you and your works closer to God. If this happens, you will be fulfilled as a professional, hoping, by faith, that the picture will come out right.

Faith demands that you challenge the *status quo*. It gives you the drive to succeed against adversity, to push and prove yourself before God. It also bears you up in failure, which you will experience in your career.

As a professional woman, you already have the talent and the drive to succeed. The biggest balancing factor of all, however, is the humanity that God gives you. So I revise what I said before. I am professionally successful through hard work, but above all through God's love and his justice acting in this world.

WOMEN LEADERSHIP

Christine Russell Lumby

Christine Russell Lumby has a degree in English, a Diploma in Social Administration from LSE, Diplomas in Adult Education and Social Work and an MA in Theology. In 1982 Christine was appointed as the first woman Diocesan Social Responsibility Officer in the Church of England, and in that role helped establish the Nottingham inter-cultural theology course CONTRAST. She still co-tutors the Old Testament module on that course. In 1991 Christine was appointed Chief Executive of Macedon, a Nottingham charity housing homeless people. Macedon achieved Investors in People status in 1997. She chairs a Diocesan Working Party to set up a Lay Ministry Training Course.

'You're good to work with Christine, you think like a man.' The year was 1970, the speaker was my Head of Department in a Polytechnic – a man of course – and I was very flattered. Now, 30 years later I would be furious and he, being 'politically correct', would not voice his opinion in that way anyway.

Women's day in leadership has come and women no longer have to emulate a male style to be accepted. Far from it! The leadership gurus whose lectures I keenly attend in an effort to be in the forefront of good practice and to pick up the top tips, all seem to agree that the guys often have to learn what comes naturally to the girls. Of course, gender generalizations invite nearly everyone to claim to be the exception or to rubbish the original assertion rather than examine them for truth. Checking out with management consultants – both men and women – they agree there is a discernible difference in the way men and women lead and organize.

So what is the difference? Out of my current experience of leading a staff of 70, in a voluntary organization where most of the Project Managers are women and which has gained its accreditation as an Investor in People, compared with my previous ten years of working in the male-dominated world of the Church of England, a number of characteristics of women's management style seem evident to me, and these have up-sides and down-sides.

Up-sides

Consensus rather than competition is one key. Women are team players, very conscious of quality of relationships within the group, putting less emphasis on 'star's' performance and more on the team's effective working. That may mean the most effort going into the weaker members, encouraging, training and coaching them to reach their maximum potential, getting fellows to help out if one is under pressure. The emphasis is on the group rather than the individual. Agreed agendas and shared goals are of paramount importance. Even if a woman strongly believes she is right she usually wants to know that others concur, especially if they are affected by her decisions. So women seem to be less autocratic than their male counterparts. They tend to encourage more feedback from their colleagues and team members and to take more note of its content in an effort to improve performance than most men would, even when its tone is negative. Because finding the solution is more important than the status of an individual, at their best, female leaders will share the responsibility for coming up with that solution with the team or group and seek the input of critics to do so.

Empowering and encouraging are the hallmarks of the most successful leaders and, because women often suffer from low self-esteem and confidence, they blossom only in the warmth of approval and wilt under the sharp blasts of criticism which, to some men, might seem bracing. If women feel affirmed they will produce their creative best, both in problem-solving and in persistent loyal effort. Carrots are the motivators, not sticks, and threats can so easily demolish a fragile self-confidence.

However, there are very few folk who cannot appreciate cause and effect, so leaders, male or female, can address unsatisfactory performance without destroying hard-won self-esteem, by getting someone to recognize the consequences of their behaviour on themselves and others. To own a personal example, my track record of punctuality was dramatically improved when a woman colleague pointed out that my message to those I kept waiting was that my time was much more important than theirs!

Values, shared or respected within the group, are a strong cohesive force, so they need to be articulated frequently and related to practice and policy at every point. Failure to 'walk the talk' when it comes to values, quickly leads to a discredited leadership, loss of integrity and reduced confidence. Maybe because of experience in child-rearing and the need for consistency in that context which many women bring to management, they are better, in my view, at not succumbing to the temptation to jettison values from the deck of expediency when the two conflict. As there tends to be less rhetoric around in women-led initiatives, challenges to the leadership about the application of agreed values can be judged on merit and taken on board if found valid, rather than be seen as a personal attack by the leader.

Designing solutions is much more important than apportioning blame when it comes to tackling problems in getting the job done, so women will multi-task, swap jobs and be very flexible when they are working really well as a group, but this will usually depend on a strong degree of trust and high morale. Creativity in problem-solving can be highly prized by women leaders even if this is not their particular gifting. Identifying the person with the gifts to address a particular problem means a team leader must know and encourage others to know each other's strengths and to sit loose to role in order to get the right person(s) working on the job. I found this essential when involved in establishing the CONTRAST course – an intercultural theology university certificate course in Nottingham, designed to enable lay people from both black and white majority churches to study together and to access some good quality adult education where a variety of Christian traditions would be respected.

Partnership and teamwork are the watchwords of modern management and leadership theory, and because women tend to be less conscious of status they are often very good at working with others in ways that nourish partnership initiatives and ecumenical ventures. These key into their desire to achieve consensus and get tasks done in a co-operative way that includes as many people as possible and over-rides competitive tendencies. Because of a practical bias, tasks are broken down into manageable chunks with everyone contributing to the team effort and volunteering to take things on that they feel comfortable doing. In my experience of setting up Christian initiatives that cut across denominational divides, women are less concerned about ideological differences and more concerned to find and build on the common ground.

Continuous learning is the hallmark of the organization on its way to excellence, and confident women leaders are committed to training for others and to their own personal learning and development, often setting themselves quite challenging targets both in formal and informal goals – to achieve qualifications and to improve the ways they and their organizations do things. Part of continuous improvement is monitoring and evaluating previous performance, and women's style for feedback may be informal, a sort of 'How do you think that went? How could it have been better?' rather than a formal evaluation questionnaire and analysis.

There are excellent training opportunities available in the secular environment which in my experience can often be accessed at a subsidized cost if I plead my cause to the organizers. Local Training and Enterprise Councils (TECs) are a tremendous resource and committed to helping the voluntary sector, including faith communities, improve their managerial skills. I and my organization, Macedon, have had a huge amount of assistance from the Greater Nottingham TEC. The voluntary sector has appropriate training events and will put on inexpensive, in-house, customized courses for a team or organization if requested.

Planning and juggling priorities are essential skills for any woman in work – paid or unpaid, part-time or full-time. Many women live lives of unutterable complexity, juggling relationship demands, house duties, financial choices, transport constraints and work commitments not only for themselves but often for dependants as well. Thinking ahead and ironing out the conflicting requirements gives first-class training for managerial tasks. In recruitment terms 'just a housewife' or 'homemaker' could get you a practised organizer and manager. It is not just the juggling feats, it is also balancing priorities with realism – the art of the possible – required to run a family which is such useful practice.

Networking is an important facet of modern senior management and needs to be developed on one's way up. It is easier for those of us who are confident, extrovert and really like talking to people. But the secret of that is to be interested in them – and women usually are, but don't like to push themselves forward. I have a number of ploys I use on myself to overcome such reticence. I know how pleased I am when someone comes to speak to me after I have given a talk or when I am at some social event. Another way of making contact with conference speakers is to ask a penetrating question and follow it up afterwards by going and speaking to them about their reply and to affirm something they said in their talk.

To go to an event with a mental checklist of people who are likely to be there that it would be useful to talk to means that even the dullest event is both enjoyable and worthwhile. If I know people who are hostile to my organization or to me I will pluck up courage to go and be as friendly and charming as I can be, but quite briefly so I don't push their tolerance! If all that sounds a bit calculating, think of it as planning for your organization's good.

Strong and caring, engendering love, loyalty and respect, women leaders at their best are superb. Their natural qualities are being identified as crucial for management by experts such as Stephen Covey, the author of a brilliant book, *The Seven Habits of Highly Effective People* (1989), which has taught me so much. They care for staff and volunteers, take notice of service users, balance vision with practicality, foster team effort from the grass roots up. As I heard it described by one management guru, they espouse the 'geese not crows' style of leadership. Geese, when migrating, share out the demanding position of lead goose, taking turns so that no one gets exhausted, travel in each other's slipstream, go back and escort weak or injured birds in the formation, two staying with any who fall to the ground until they die or recover, before rejoining their own or another skein. Crows, on the other hand, are always squabbling about who is the top crow and do not co-operate as a group to enhance their corporate strength. Women find it easier to be geese because they are less competitive than many men.

So much for the up-side, but sadly there is a down-side too.

Down-side

Too focused on personalities, the woman leader can be too accommodating of the individuals in her team and to modify plans around them. This may sacrifice long-term ends to meet short-term needs. Accepting of human limitations in others, sometimes because of acute awareness of her own shortcomings, a woman leader can be so conscious of another's needs or circumstances that she cannot hold boundaries effectively. In extreme cases this will prevent, or delay, the discipline or removal of a disruptive team member whose attitude is having a profoundly negative effect on everyone around them.

Loss of nerve and self-confidence when things go wrong and the critics, particularly the male ones, are on the prowl seeking a victim to sacrifice on the altar of blame, can easily cause a woman to waiver in her resolve. In my observation and experience I and other older women tend to regard male expertise a little too highly – as we were brought up to do – and we tend to wilt or become defensive in the face of strong male challenge. 'A Cinderella complex' of self-doubt can bring up inappropriate responses, like tears, in the most awkward of places – committees or public meetings! The roots of these feelings have to be dealt with well away from the arenas where the symptoms may show themselves and require us to examine some of our deepest assumptions about ourselves and significant others' evaluations of us – usually made way back in the past. Neuro-Linguistic Programming (NLP) courses may be useful in dealing with these, as can counselling or simply remembering some of the things said to us as children, or the models we were given by our mothers, by our other relatives or by other role models which have dented our confidence or stunted our proper self-esteem.

Over-demanding of self and others in an unrealistic struggle to please causes many women extreme stress. They make heroic efforts to complete work in impossible deadlines or to cope with far too much work and too few resources in circumstances where many men would protest and down tools. This character-istic can make women just as difficult bosses as men if they inspire loyal devotion in their team who do not want to disap-point or let them down. 'I'm just a gal who can't say no, I'm in a terrible fix!' is not a good signature tune for a leader or her team. But it's one I've had to learn to stop singing, at least when it involves my staff in unrealistic workloads or where my perfor-mance is being adversely affected by my self-induced overload. Women usually want to please and to receive approval, so we are suckers for the 'Could you possibly just squeeze this in for me?' line when the answer should be a firm 'No, sorry, not this time.'

Too personal in our perspective, especially if things are going wrong, we feel it's our fault, or that others are blaming us or our judgement when they are usually just voicing their opinions. It's a big step forward in our calibre as a leader when we can encour-age people to express views that sound critical without feeling threatened, becoming defensive or keeling over in capitulation to a strongly expressed alternative. Women often need to work on the techniques of listening openly in a relaxed way. I found the insights of Paul Bridle of Proaction International very helpful in this regard. Paul has studied the characteristics of hundreds of successful top leaders and found that they nurture champions in their teams, are never threatened by having people far more able than themselves in their teams, and that they encourage the open expression of views even when strongly at odds with their own! When all members of a team have a chance to have a say, they are much more likely to own the final decision made and we can drive for the best solutions rather than bow to the loudest criticisms.

Gill Taylor of Connections Partnerships, another manage-ment consultant and trainer with extensive experience in the voluntary and not-for-profit sector, whose opinion I respect enormously, says that women leaders are too quick to doubt their own judgement and change course when they come under fire, but if they hold steady they usually make good decisions and inspire confidence in those who work with and for them. It is good in such circumstances to check out issues with a respected colleague or two, and test the waters.

There are times, however, when one should not be afraid to change one's mind rather than stick with a poor decision or one made without full information. When I do find myself persuaded to change my mind, I find it useful to let all parties affected by the change know the reasons as soon as possible so that they have heard it from me first and can question me or respond to me personally if they do not agree. No leader gets it right every time or gets colleagues' agreement even when they have, so be easy on yourself when you don't. Forgive yourself, as you forgive others.

Fear of change and lack of confidence in oneself to handle it often causes women not to seek leadership roles or to accept it when offered. I am glad to see this rarely happens among younger women who have grown up in the atmosphere of equality. However, I observe that women less often equip themselves for senior management by getting qualifications, volunteer to lead a venture or seek practice in the skills of the Board meeting than do their male counterparts.

What about the Christian dimension? Does it make a difference?

Yes, it does. Sad though this is to admit, life is more difficult for Christian women leaders in churches or other Christian contexts. The Church lags behind the secular world in its appreciation of women's particular contribution to organizational development.

The doctrine and tradition of some Christian denominations mean that the right of any woman to be in a position of leadership or authority over men, or a mix of men and women, is in question or is openly prohibited. So it is not an unusual experience for an able, young, black or white woman to be encouraged in her secular job or to aspire to the highest echelons of management because her abilities are recognized and cherished, while in her church life she is expected to defer to disabling, domineering male leaders of far less skill and experience just because they are men and she a woman!

Even in churches which pride themselves on not being sexist, assumptions are openly expressed about the male right to lead which would not be tolerated in a half-decent equal opportunities employment situation. If she challenges this in the way considered desirable in the secular environment, the female church member may well be accused of having an attitude problem to authority. I was once accused of being 'the sort of woman who was ruining the Church of England' when I questioned, as politely and non-threateningly as I could, the use of the word 'brethren' repeatedly inserted into the liturgy of a service where there were more women present than men.

If not excluded from formal leadership roles, a woman may find that there are expectations that she will be content to exercise a supporting ministry and not go on to seek the top job where, however collaborative or inclusive her style, she would have to take authority from time to time.

Women have to find a non-threatening style to challenge such attitudes and to engage their fellow church members, both men and women, in the debate. Quite a lot of careful education in gender issues, inclusive language and the like, can be sabotaged by women who have gladly embraced sexist teaching as gospel and who declare themselves perfectly content to be an invisible subset of men and permanently under their control and direction. Women will not win this battle on their own: they need sympathetic male colleagues within the leadership who will express their belief in the justness of their cause. They can be found among those who are employed in places of work where diversity is valued and equal opportunities are upheld. Other supporters may be found who have experienced exclusion on other grounds – race or class or faith.

Where the subjugation of women is upheld on the basis of biblical authority it is harder to dislodge. Here challenging scripture with scripture may be useful.

As many of you as were baptised into Christ have clothed yourself with Christ. There is no longer Jew nor Greek, there is no longer slave or free, there is no longer male and female; for all of you are one in Christ Jesus. (Galatians 3:27–29, NRSV)

There is evidence that this credal statement about the equality of men and women was the one that the early male Christians, being devout Jews or normally sexist Greeks, found more unpalatable than tolerating each other's cultures or socio-economic divisions and, what is more, one they could easily agree with each other about. So it was probably the first to be dropped from practice within this Spirit-filled community where the three great divisions of society from time immemorial – race, status and gender – had been overthrown because of their new understanding of the kingdom of God.

Now, the non-believing Western world, having absorbed the Christian belief that all human beings are of equal worth and value, is living out this understanding with more integrity than some faith communities who, though they say that God creates and loves all his children equally, continue to deny that faith in the way they act around the leadership rights of women, members with disabilities or who come from ethnic minorities or have low economic or social status.

Biblical models

The first recorded model of management through team building appears in the Bible when the over-stressed Moses was given some excellent advice by Jethro, his father-in-law, acting as his management consultant, to delegate responsibility to a team of able leaders who would administer law and adjudicate in disputes. Jethro pointed out that Moses was burning himself out, trying to be a control-freak and ignoring his real role as trainer, leader and negotiator with God (Exodus 18:14–23, NRSV). This passage merits in-depth study by any Christian in leadership. It contains inspired wisdom. God appears to endorse the same model when Moses again was under intense pressure because folk had got fed up with their diet of manna and were blaming Moses; he in turn was blaming God – a sure sign of poor management methods and a stressed managing director.

> So the Lord said to Moses, 'Gather for me seventy of the elders of Israel . . . I will come down and talk with you there and I will take some of the spirit that is on you and put it on them: and they shall bear the burden of the people along with you so that you will not bear it all by yourself.' (Numbers 11:10–17, NRSV)

Jesus, as was customary for a Rabbi aiming to lead a renewal movement within Judaism, chose twelve members for his immediate team and 70 more from his wider discipleship to train up in his unique mission and ministry methods. Jesus encouraged women and did not write them off as theological and spiritual nonentities, as was often the custom of his day. As a result they were devoted to him and his cause and gave their all for him. Within the group who travelled with Jesus there were a number of women, including some who financially supported him – a support which Jesus appeared to accept gracefully. 'The twelve were with him, as well as some women . . . and many others, who provided for them out of their own resources' (Luke 8:1–3, NRSV).

Gender agenda

Those are the models of management in the Bible, but what of the issue of biblical authorization for women's leadership? There are not many instances, but there are inspirations and they are not dealt with as oddities. Miriam, Deborah, Judith, Esther provided significant leadership to the Jews in critical situations. Mary Magdalene is believed to have taken the Gospel to India along with Thomas. Then there were all those women house-church leaders mentioned so warmly by Paul in his letters.

In church history women have played an important role in

founding or building up religious communities which have found new ways of exemplifying Christ – in mission, service and worship. Hildegard, Clare, Hilda of Whitby, Teresa of Avila and a huge host of other saintly women have worked tirelessly among the disadvantaged and excluded – poor, sick, disabled, abused, homeless, uneducated, children, elderly, in every continent and generation, serving their Lord as they serve these. Ask anyone on the street to name a famous Christian of our day, and Mother Theresa of Calcutta is likely to come up often among those mentioned.

And what characterizes their ministry? They established groups to work together in a supportive way and they empowered and encouraged the women and the men who worked with them, so that the initiative continued after they had bowed out. The test of a collaborative style is that it raises up others to take over when the pioneer has to step down as leader.

My personal experience as a woman in Christian leadership

I have been blessed in receiving a clear mandate from God for the leadership roles he has called me into, and this has been particularly important to recollect when the going has been rough – that he chose me as a woman to do that job knowing how well or badly I would perform in certain aspects of it. When I was appointed as Southwell Diocesan Social Responsibility Officer I was the first woman in the Church of England to hold such a post and the first lay appointee in that job in our Diocese, so I desperately wanted to make a good job of it for the sake of women's good name.

It was quite lonely being the only woman at meetings, and this was intensified when I was the only lay person present. I had to trust that God knew that my theology would be good enough and that he knew that I had a useful contribution to make out of my experience as a lay woman hitherto employed in secular environments. I kept reminding myself, and occasionally my colleagues, that Jesus was a lay person and that he had problems too with the religious leaders of his day, especially about his authority for leadership! I must say my immediate colleagues and episcopal line management were incredibly supportive and loving, even when I was brash and acerbic.

What was really difficult, was coming to work in a Christian environment from a secular social work one and finding it, compared to the non-Christian one, so sexist and unknowingly, unthinkingly, oppressive to women. It seemed that each woman had to battle for recognition against prejudice and only won it for herself – never for her sisters as well. Glass ceilings took the form of solid vaulted roofs in the Church in the 1980s, but that is changing slowly, praise God. We have to keep raising the issues of exclusion and not let the churches use tradition and often poor theological or biblical understanding to duck out of their oppressive practices and sexist language. It is a matter of mission. Present members may be tolerant and forgiving, but new converts will not be. Why should they when the Church is supposed to demonstrate the kingdom?

I am now back in secular employment as the chief executive of a housing association and registered charity which provides supported accommodation for homeless people; but my organization, Macedon, had a Christian foundation and still enjoys tremendous Christian support. That takes me into 50 different churches of all different denominations each year and it is exciting to see what God is achieving through his women disciples. They lead many of the most thriving, well-run churches which have a significant outreach into their local communities.

When a team or organization is headed up by a woman it is easier for her to develop a culture in which both women and men will flourish and grow. It is much harder for her to do this in an environment dominated by male styles and assumptions. My experience is that in that situation the woman needs to build an empowered team who work in this way and, from the position of proven performance (which will surely appear), she can, with credibility, make suggestions to improve the functioning of other areas of the institution.

A few working principles

- Keep the vision of excellence in the forefront of everyone's thinking.
- Inspire a sense of shared responsibility and ownership.
- Encourage people daily by affirmation, praise, interest and asking their opinion.
- Listen to and put others' good ideas into practice and give credit where due.
- Learn from secular training and seize all development opportunities available.
- Nurture champions in one's team and network; they are a strength, not a threat.
- Establish partnership, collaboration and consultation.
- Like and value people, and let them see it.
- Make the work as enjoyable and fulfilling as possible for self and others.
- Go for it; for God is with you, sister!

References

Covey, Stephen R. (1989) *The Seven Habits of Highly Effective People: Restoring the Character Ethic*, London: Simon & Schuster.

Dowling, Colette (1981) *The Cinderella Complex: Women's Hidden Fear of Independence*, London: Joseph.

Manning, Marilyn and Haddock, Patricia (1989) *Leadership Skills for Women*, London: Kogan Page.

Sprinkle, Patricia H. (1992) *Women Who Do Too Much: Stress and the Myth of the Superwoman*, New York: Harper Paperbooks.

CULTURAL SPIRITUAL RECOVERY:
A BLACK WOMAN'S EXPERIENCE
IN THE CHURCH

Janet Johnson

Janet Johnson was born in England and her parents originate from the West Indies. She currently works at the University of Central England as a Senior Lecturer in Finance and Accounting. She considers herself to be a 'Bapticostal' although she was nurtured and baptized at Small Heath Baptist Church in Birmingham, where she currently is a member. For the past five years she has been visiting and worshipping with the congregation at Church of God of Prophecy at Cattell Road in Small Heath. She is interested in youth work and is currently in the process of establishing a Saturday School for children in the Small Heath area in conjunction with other youth workers in the area. Janet enjoys reading, listening to an array of music from gospel to R & B, keeping fit by running and working out at the gym, writing poetry, and socializing with friends.

Life is a journey made up of a series of adventures and lessons that are incredulously intertwined by our Creator to imbue us with the vast array of knowledge we need to acquire, so that we as individuals become all that we are predestined to be and thereby maximize our potential.

In this chapter I shall endeavour to share with you how being a woman in the Church has affected my life's journey. My entire existence has been determined by the fact that I chose Jesus as my paradigm and decided to emulate his life. Jesus has vividly helped me to understand who I am and why I am here, and has given me the faith and confidence to believe that I can become anything I want to be.

To me Jesus embellishes all that is positive. Once I let him into my heart the insidious nebulosity that permeated my path was lifted. The elucidation of how this happened is a process of enlightenment and discovery that is still in progress. I believe this evolvement and learning curve will be a perpetual one; indeed I sincerely hope so, because once the truth is revealed in minuscule fragments, one desires a complete revelation to follow.

Retrospective analysis of my explorative journey thus far has led me to acknowledge that, from the myriad of adventures and lessons I have encountered, my mien has been transformed as I experienced two radical reawakenings in the Church, that have facilitated me as I've searched for liberation, self-identity and self-redemption.

However, I need to divulge some information about the many worlds I inhabit. First and foremost I am a Christian. I am also proud to say that I am a black African Caribbean woman. Despite the fact that I am a lecturer, I consider myself to be a student, because the pedagogy of life is eternal. Lastly I am a poet; and bearing all this in mind, I shall endeavour to tell my story by converging the antithetical worlds of science, art and religion.

The first radical reawakening took place when I was sixteen. A cataclysmic event occurred: I had a spiritual rebirth. There were no bright lights or flashing symbols. Having grown up in a Christian home, I made a personal decision to follow Jesus. There was a conviction within my spirit that enabled me to recognize that I had to awaken from the oblivion and darkness around me; I realized there had to be an abnegation of my old life and, as it says in Romans 12:2, 'A renewing of my mind' took place – I had seen the light.

This is a process that we all need to go through. We are all spiritual beings, and entrenched within the inner recesses of our souls is an unrelenting desire to be reconnected to the supreme spiritual being – our Father God. I found this connection through Jesus. To me Jesus epitomized love, and that was precisely what I needed.

When I talk about love it has to be contextualized, and the words of 1 Corinthians 13 say it all. This is what Jesus exemplifies for me:

Love is very patient and kind, never jealous or envious, never boastful or proud, never haughty or selfish or rude. Love does not demand its own way. It is not irritable or touchy. It does not hold grudges and will hardly even notice when others do it wrong. It is never glad about injustice, but rejoices whenever truth wins out. If you love someone you will be loyal to him no matter what the cost. You will always believe in him, always expect the best of him, and always stand your ground in defending him. There are three things that remain – faith, hope and love – and the greatest of these is love. (4–7, 13, LB)

The significance of Jesus in my life is reflected in this beautiful passage. Jesus epitomizes love for me because if one was to paraphrase the above and place his name wherever love is mentioned, the greatness of his mien begins to shine through.

The culmination of my beliefs led to my baptism, which was the most momentous day of my life. It was on a warm July evening that my elder sister and I sat as advocates of Christ. My grandmother sat with and encouraged my sister, and my mother presided over me. So gathered together on that memorable day were three generations of African queens. Undoubtedly flash-backs of their own baptisms would have permeated the thoughts of my mother and grandmother. The Church and thus Jesus had nurtured, strengthened and supported my forebears, and it would do the same for me and my sister.

African queens have a lot to contend with, and Jesus is the fulcrum of our fortitude and resilience. As Jacqueline Grant stresses,

Black women's questions about Jesus Christ are not about the relation of His humanity to His divinity or about the relation of the historical Jesus to the Christ of Faith . . . Jesus is their mother, their father, their sister and their brother. Jesus is whoever Jesus has to be to function in a supportive way in the struggle. (1989, p. 212)

Indeed, many struggles were to come in my life. My mother and grandmother had endured numerous obstacles, but on reflection the day I walked through the waters of baptism, having become cognisant of my sin, and abnegated my old life to espouse a new one, I effectively began to awaken from my apoplexy and appreciate the reason why my parents and grandparents were staunch believers in the Christian faith.

So that's why:

I want to take you back down memory lane
To a little island surrounded by fame,
There are sun-kissed mountains and golden sands
Coconut trees and steel bands.
Salt-fish, ackee, and rice and peas,
Heavenly food to put you at your ease,
Jerk pork and chicken, fruit juice and ice
Mangoes, green bananas yes it's all very nice
Good music, dominoes, cane sugar and spice,
You can relax and sip your cool drink with ice,
There's no snow or cold winds to chill your feet,
No worrying about where you are going to get your heat,
No icy footpaths and foggy nights,
Just sunshine good food and wonderful sights.

So why did our parents leave this paradise?,
To come to a place that's not so nice,
Come to a place across land so far,
Where heaven help you if you've got no car.
Cause when the winter comes and your hands start freeze,
When you catch nuff cold and you can't stop sneeze,
It's then you'll sit down with face vex and tight,
And think to yourself that they had no right,
To leave nice nice J.A. and come to a land,
Where it's so cold and icy you can't even stand.

So why did they do it?

They left that land of beauty for us,
They left with a friend in whom they could trust,
With God's help they've worked hard for their kids and we
Must not let them down please try and see,
Cause they never did it for us to drop out of school
To stand a street corner and act like fool,
To gwarn like we got no sense in a we head
And to follow a path where we might end up dead.

They may not have had much money in life
They may have worked seven days a week to cope
    with their strife,
But they showed us a way which was the best way of all,
A way to which their forebears had been called
Cause when morning came and Jim Reeves licked me ears,
And the smell of fried chicken drifted up the stairs,
I knew it was Sunday and I had to get up,
To get ready and quickly drink one hot cup.

Now when I was younger I wanted to stay in me bed,
To listen to music and make it mash up me head,
But there was no arguing or contention in my mother's
    house,
You either went to church or you heard her shout,

But the day I met Christ that's when I knew,
Why they had the courage to start anew,
They wanted the best for their kids you see,
They showed us God but for their family,
They wanted opportunity and a better life
Education, good housing and not so much strife.

You see if it wasn't for Jesus I wouldn't be here now
Coping with life I don't know how,
No friend has ever been so dear and true
And He's waiting for all of you,
If you haven't done so to let Him into your life
His love has no bounds and reaches untold heights

They came to this country where they met,
God's English family who on this land had been set,
So today we are a nation of different colours and creeds,
But we are brothers and sisters and God is all we need,
So when they are sending you to church believe me it's
        good,
Don't rebel and follow the ways of the hood,
Seek God, try your best, show them nuff respect,
It's only then as one nation will we achieve success. Amen

(Johnson, 1999b, p. 7, copyright)

Yes, I'm so glad I was sent to church. My mother knew what was best, and as the poem states, they had to be strong; my forebears had to have faith, they left paradise and settled in a place that must have seemed like hell itself. Just as the mighty women in my family embarked on a new life when they crossed the perilous waters into unknown territory, I knew nothing about what lay ahead, but I was acquiescent of the fact that, having passed through the waters of baptism, Jesus would supply me with the power I so desperately needed.

There is no doubt in my mind that Jesus has been doing this for black women for many generations. One might be tempted to think that black women are doubly disadvantaged, because we have to face the twin oppressive evils of racism and sexism.

However, this is not the case. The illustration of this is formulated in a simple mathematical law. Here, religion and science converge to form a cohesive paradigm wherein their antithetical properties are integrated. In maths, two negatives make a positive. In Christ, two attributes the world may consider negative, make a resounding positive.

This is the reality of the sublime energy that was deposited in the vault of my soul. Whenever the Spirit of God touches anything, power and positivity is the irrevocable consequence. Jesus began to deal with the negativity that had accumulated in my psyche. I truly believe that the Church is not a building or a denomination. These facets of religion are man-made artefacts which are of minimal importance. Church is within every human being. The nexus of the Holy Spirit with our own spirits creates churches that are invincible.

Therefore my church needed to be purged and renewed for me to be truly born again. The negativity had to go. My egotism was changed to altruism, my stubbornness to open-mindedness, my prejudice to acceptance and my selfishness to unconditional love. This process of regeneration is an ongoing one which only takes place as I spend time with my Lord. Through daily devotions and prayer I am able to survive whatever life throws at me.

I'm not going to disillusion you and give the misguided opinion that my life has been problem-free since I established Jesus as Lord of my life. Indeed, the opposite could be said to be true. What I can truly declare though, is that Jesus continuously supports me and strengthens me through times of benevolence and malevolence, and the word of God forever remains true:

Faith is the substance of things hoped for, the evidence of things not yet seen. (Hebrews 11:1, KJV)

Whatsoever ye shall ask the Father in my name, he will give it you. Hitherto have ye asked nothing in my name: ask and ye shall receive, that your joy may be full. (John 16:23–24, KJV)

He meant it; my life has been literally transformed. By faith he got me through my 'A' levels, university and subsequent studies, and as my elder sister has jokingly reminded me time and time again, 'Janet, it must be Jesus because I know you and it definitely is not you.' Many a true word is said in jest!

My aspirations now are unlimited; God's word states that *all* things are possible, not *some*. So, as I stressed earlier, I can be whatever I want to be, as we all can. It's through knowing Jesus that this truth has been revealed to me, and that's why:

I love Him more than words can say,
That's why I seek His face every day
I love Him more than words can say,
My Jesus my Saviour that's why I pray,

That He will always stay in my heart,
And His spirit shall never from me depart,
That my soul will always be wrapped in His love,
And my being will stay as pure as a dove.

Cause I love Him more than words can say
That's why I seek His face every day,
I love Him more than words can say
My Jesus my Saviour because He plays,

Such a wonderful part in my life
He helps me to cope with trouble and strife,
My Jesus, my Saviour, my Friend my all,
I know you'll never ever let me fall.

That's why I love Him more than words can say,
And so I seek His face every day,
I love Him more than words can say,
My Jesus my Saviour please with me stay.

(Johnson, 1999b, p. 20, copyright)

The poem says it all, I can add no more. But despite my faith
and fortitude, a period of darkness enshrouded me. You see,
having achieved a great deal educationally, I began to look
around the church environment I'd grown up in, and a murky,
insidious mass of emptiness was apparent. The Lord had done
so much for me I desired to do more for him, but on surveying
the roles open to women in the Church, I began to think that
any progression within this somewhat bureaucratic, institutionalized system of the Baptist world was remote.

Apart from that, I felt as though a huge segment of my
persona was missing. I mechanically performed my duties of

Sunday School teacher and youth leader, but my zeal and enthusiasm were absent. Inevitably my spirit retreated, I became languid and apathetic, I was drying up as quickly as water would do in an arid desert. I seemed to be experiencing a nullification of the feelings I had towards my church, and my faith was being annihilated. As this state of emptiness and starvation ensued, I went through a period where I suffered from a profound spiritual marasmus.

We all go through valleys as well as reaching the higher echelons of mountain-tops, and this valley was deep and lonely. To the outside world I oozed success and yet I felt void and empty, but God's word does not return void. He tells us:

> Ask and it shall be given you, seek and ye shall find, knock and it shall be opened unto you. For everyone that asketh receiveth, and he that seeketh findeth, and to him that knocketh the door shall be opened. (Matthew 7:7–8)

I asked God to help me and by an incredulous series of events I ended up at a black Pentecostal church. Amen, praise the Lord, Hallelujah! This was what I needed. I remember the very first sermon I heard there as if it were yesterday. A mature Caribbean gentleman preached from Matthew 5:13, where Jesus talks about us being the salt of the earth. He stated God's word and then in broad patois he shouted 'So brethren, you all better salt up all you self for 1996.' These simple words were said in a dialect I could identify with and there and then it clicked. The second cataclysmic reawakening took place, and this was the beginning of my cultural rebirth. For the whole of my Christian life I had grown up in a religious setting that showed me nothing concerning who I was. I sought, and indeed I found out, that God is not a man that he should lie. I recognized that I had to release myself from the negative, stereotypical images that had bombarded my mind. I needed to be liberated from the mental shackles that were impeding my progress. I'd spiritually grown up in a church culture characterized by a predominantly white patriarchal system. There is nothing wrong with this, but God's word says 'God created human beings in his own image, in the image of God he created them' (Genesis 1:27), and I realized that this truth had been literally eradicated from my life. Our Father is a truly holistic Father and he is concerned with every aspect of our being. He desires for us 'To prosper and be in good health even as our souls prosper' (3 John 2). The verse is not speaking only of material health but also our physical, mental and spiritual health.

I needed to know who I was, my mind had become impregnated with lies which, if I did not take effective steps to obliterate them, would give birth to a child of deception that would leave me going nowhere.

The truths of God's word became excitingly real. I recognized that I was 'fearfully and wonderfully made' (Psalm 139:14) and so I needed to re-educatate myself and learn about my culture, my African heritage and my black history. By ignoring these crucial aspects of my life I was rejecting all that God had done for me. I was resigned to know the truth, because it was only the truth that would set me free.

The encounter that I had with my culture in a church setting where I sensed a powerful affiliation with the people around me literally changed my spiritual life. I did not leave the Baptist world into which I had been nurtured, but encapsulated both of them into my life. God has been showing me that we, as Christ's Body, are one. When we rise above our ephemeral differences, abnegate our outdated prejudicial shibboleths and realize the massive potential that the Church has when it operates as a cohesive unit, magnanimous things will begin to happen.

Being a woman in the Church, I've already stressed that I now acknowledge that my Church is within me, but I want to see power reverberating through the very core of Christ's Body and ultimately society itself. When we recognize we are one, God's power will manifest over and above our individual cultural, sexual and racial hang-ups.

With the onset of my second reawakening, the journey of life had taken a positive uphill course, and to aid me in my vigorous pursuits God sent many teachers and nurturers along my path who directed me to the world of black theology, black literature and black history. These tripartite facets of my culture opened up a whole new world of liberation and intellectualism for me, which easily penetrated my soul because I could readily identify with the principles and feelings involved.

Black theology was the harbinger of them all. This ideology was pioneered and promulgated by Professor James Cone, who has been described as the 'founding father' of black theology. He defines it thus: 'Black theology is a theology of and for black people, an examination of their stories, tales and sayings. It is an investigation of the mind into the raw materials of our pilgrimage, telling the story of "how we got over"' (Cone, 1975, p. 18).

It is a philosophy that effectively combines remnants of the Black Power movement of America with Christian theology, and it has been described as a 'liberation theology'. Truly this is the case; Jesus himself declared that he had come to set captives free, and I knew that I had to be released from the chains that were binding me. As I began to explore the Bible and acknowledge that many characters in there were black, I realized how brainwashed and traumatized I was. Why? This truth gradually dawned on me. I consider God to be my Father, as he is the Father of us all. In parts of South Africa, until recently relatively few children would have seen a white person, therefore if you explained the Gospel to them and asked them to draw an image of God, undoubtedly they would produce a black image, because they are black. To my shame and disgust I realized that until my mind had been liberated by black theology, I would have portrayed my Father as white.

God made all of us in his image, so I believe that he's black, white, red and whatever colour individuals perceive him to be. This confusion has to be annihilated from our conscience, so as James Cone correctly states:

The task of Black Theology then is to analyse the nature of the gospel of Jesus Christ in the light of oppressed blacks so that they will see the gospel as inseparable from their humiliated condition, and as bestowing on them the necessary power to break the chains of oppression. (1970, p. 1)

All black people in the Church need to recognize this truth, and as they are empowered, this truth will begin to set them free too.

I must move on to the second ingredient in this wonderful cocktail of self-redemption. Discovering black literature was like receiving manna from heaven. I love reading and, for the greater part of my life I'd perused the works of Jane Austen, the Brontë sisters, Dickens and Shakespeare – to name a few. These are all excellent authors who thrilled and continue to thrill my mind. However, when my teachers revealed the books written by Maya Angelou, Alice Walker, Zora Neale Hurston, W. E. B. Du Bois and James Baldwin, I could scarcely contain myself.

The autobiographical works of Maya Angelou ooze with courage and inspiration. She is a truly positive role model for all women who are under the mistaken belief that God has not endowed us with a perpetual source of power. The fact that she was a single mother at the age of sixteen but still struggled, fought and aspired to a position in which she was asked to perform her poetry at President Clinton's inauguration, is mind blowing. She clearly shows how, with God, confidence and self-determination, all things are possible. As she herself has written:

> You may write me down in history
> With you bitter twisted lies,
> You may trod me in the very dirt
> But still like dust I'll rise. (Maya, 1995)

Jane Austen and the Brontë sisters did not inspire me to such depths, and as I began to reflect on my education, I became angry. Why was I not told of these authors at school? If God had not opened the doors that had been cleverly locked through my mis-education, I would never have heard of these extremely talented scribes. We must be our own educators. God provides everything for his children; I asked for wisdom and guidance and he gave it to me through the medium of his messengers. Whatever we learn – if it has empowered us, we must share it with others to facilitate their learning, I'm so glad that my teachers practised this rule.

The last ingredient of sustenance in my cultural diet is the world of black history. When I was at school I had no interest in William the Conqueror, the Normans and the Saxons. Reminiscing on my historical education, the only aspect of black history that I was taught was slavery. It's only in the last four years that I have found out about black heroes such as Mary Seacole, Harriet Tubman and Booker T. Washington, to name a few. Of course I'd heard about and indeed studied in great depth the life and works of Martin Luther King Jr and Malcolm X – but that was all.

It is of paramount importance that we have positive role models, both contemporary and historic, so that we have the knowledge and confidence to rise above the negative, one-sided view portrayed by slavery. We need to know that our forefathers built educational and cultural institutions, because armed with this information we will realize that we are not destined to be bound in shackles, but like all people, God predestined us for excellence and he desires for us to maximize our potential. Knowledge of one's history and culture breeds confidence and, as the great Marcus Garvey stated, 'If you have no confidence in self, you are twice defeated in the race of life. With confidence, you have won even before you have started' (Vanzant, 1993, p. 38).

These three facets of my second reawakening had a poignant effect on me. I was so glad that God did hear my cry and attend to my prayer. I am now truly awake, but there is a lot more to learn; as more and more minuscule fragments of negativity fall away from my eyes I am catching a tiny glimpse of what being a child of God is all about. I am proud that I am a black Christian woman and I thank God daily for all that he has shown me and is continually revealing to me. I know I have the power and the confidence to become all that God wants me to be.

In conclusion, I'd like to leave you with the words of a very powerful Christian woman and a poem that I hope will inspire you. Coretta Scott, the wife of Martin Luther King, said the following when interviewed by Alice Walker:

The black woman has a special role to play. Our heritage of suffering and our experience in having to struggle against

101

all odds to raise our children gives us a greater capacity for understanding both suffering and the need and meaning of compassion. When you look at what some black women have gone through, and then look at how beautiful they still are it is incredible that they still believe in the values of race and that they have retained a love of justice. This is a kind of miracle, something we must preserve and must pass on. (Walker, 1993, pp. 152–3)

Miracles are works of God alone. It is only because I am a woman in the Church that this miracle has begun in me and I urge you to allow the same process to take place in your hearts too. Lastly, sisters with power should always acknowledge the following.

> We are dark majestic and beautiful and we must remember that
> We have been given by our Creator the wonderful colour black,
> Throughout ages past and present us African queens have grown
> And many a seed of wisdom and love we have sown.
> Where shall I start? With whom shall I begin?
> Let me remind you of the soul sisters who are our kin.
> The Queen of Sheba and Cleopatra is where I shall commence,
> Whose beauty and presence I'm told was immense,
> Other Queens of the Nile have come forth from Africa,
> And carried forth messages of joy, peace and wonder.
> Harriet Tubman, Mahalia Jackson and Rosa Parkes are others,
> Who have taken a stand and inspired their sisters and their brothers,
> Alice Walker, Oprah and of course Maya Angelou,
> Have shown what self respect and determination can do.
> Let me dwell on Maya for a short little while,
> To explain why that sister has got such courage and style.
> Time and time they knocked her down but like a phoenix she did arise,

And elegantly brushed herself down and reached for the
   skies,
Nothing could tame her spirit, nothing would make her lie,
Within the depths of despair and sit down and cry.
So you can see,
That strong majestic and beautiful is how they had to be,
And those God given qualities abide in you and me.
Our mothers, sisters and grandmothers are all African
   queens,
And the ancestral spirit inside us all does teem,
Yes, Africa the Motherland the birth place of us all,
Should always be inside our hearts and we can always call
Upon our Creator who to us has so much endowed,
Yes queens keep your eyes on Him and walk tall and straight
   and proud. Amen!

(Johnson, 1999a, copyright)

References

Angelou, Maya (1995) *Maya Angelou: the Complete Collected Poems*,
   London: Virago Press.
Cone, James (1970) *A Black Theology of Liberation*, New York: Lippincott.
Cone, James (1975) *God of the Oppressed*, San Francisco: Harper.
Grant, Jacqueline (1989) *White Women's Christ*, Atlanta: Scholars Press.
Johnson, Janet (1999a) *Rhapsodies in Black*, unpublished works of the Con-
   scious Poets Society.
Johnson, Janet (1999b) *To be Loved: the Reason Why*, Feather Books.
Vanzant, Iyanla (1993) *Acts of Faith*, New York: Simon and Schuster.
Walker, Alice (1993) *In Search of our Mothers' Gardens*, Harcourt, Brace
   Jovanovich.

BEING A MINISTER'S WIFE

Sandra Ackroyd

Sandra Ackroyd currently lives in Tottenham, North London, and is married to a United Reformed Church minister. They have three children and are also guardians to young asylum seekers. Sandra's current job involves working with issues facing urban United Reformed Churches (URC) in north and south London, as part-time co-ordinator of the Urban Churches Support Group. Previously Sandra spent several years as Youth and Children's Work Trainer of the Thames North Synod (URC). She has also spent time in campaign and training work with racial justice programmes and initiatives. As well as time with family and the local church, Sandra enjoys spending time with friends, seeing a good film or show, and having the occasional holiday in the sun – especially a Greek island!

Sandra did not grow up in the context of a church family (nuclear or extended), but was sent to a local Congregational Church (later to become URC) with a neighbour when she was six years old. Since her teens Sandra has received many opportunities by and with the Church (locally, regionally, nationally and internationally) and she is grateful to God for these experiences. She extends this gratitude to the many people who led her to take up such opportunities and for travelling with her on her life and faith journey.

I have now been a minister's wife for 30 years. Being asked to write about this experience has been a real challenge for me, because it is the least role I have in my life that I ever think about. Maybe the reasons for this will unravel themselves as the chapter progresses. In this story I shall speak of expectations, relationships, ministries, choices, tradition, culture, faith and the Church. As I write I will move between the private and public realms of life. Also, I shall be as honest as I can be, and hope that this process of reflection will be helpful and encouraging for other readers and myself.

Speaking of expectations of a minister's wife, I need to mention my own expectations, those of my husband, and those of the congregations and even communities. I shall begin by sharing my experiences of the first church where my husband was minister. It was a small church, called Heaton Way United Reformed Church, on a large housing estate (Harold Hill, Romford, Essex). In this community most people did not have a track record of churchgoing and the church was less than ten years old. It only had the experience of one previous minister, and she was a single woman. Therefore this church had no experience or expectations of a minister's wife. On arriving at this church we were met with some stark realities in the community, one characteristic being that it was teaming with young people and children. One of the first things my husband and I were asked to do, maybe because we were just 25 years old and because I had previous experience in youth work, was to tackle different aspects of work with young people, including starting an 'open' youth club. As time went by, I began to see a voluntary ministry of my own emerging within the local church among young people and children. I also encouraged other leaders in the work. The fact that I was a minister's wife was not a factor or an issue, and I was very comfortable with this. From the beginning of our time in this first church, as far as the congregation was concerned, I was seen, and in fact saw myself, as an ordinary church member sharing the gifts God had given me and developing the skills I had acquired. However, I detected a few assumptions about ministers and spouses in encounters with people not connected to the church. On two different occasions a person came to the door and asked to speak to the vicar (i.e. minister). Each time they also said 'May I speak to your dad?' Was there an idea here that a minister and spouse had to belong to a particular age group? Did these people hold an image in their heads of a bald-headed ageing man and a wife who would look similar? I would like to add that I am two months older than my husband! On another occasion, when I was walking to Romford shopping centre with my first child, an elderly woman and member of the Romford United Reformed Church, asked 'How are you getting on in that terrible place, dear?' She was referring to our housing estate where we were living. In the early years of the life of the estate, which was twenty years ago, this woman could remember that there had been gang fights there. Clearly this did not still happen, but she assumed it was a bad and dangerous place in which to be, and how would I, as a young minister's wife, be coping? I sensed her care and kindness, but she could also be making an inappropriate assumption about my own background and experience.

For me, being a minister's wife was only significant in the relationship between my husband and myself. What were our expectations of the role of a minister's wife? Both of us worked towards mutual support in relation to his work and mine within the local church and community. During the early years I had to learn a great deal of patience when my husband wanted me to listen to every sermon and talk before he delivered them. However, this changed as he became more confident and when our children were born.

When we moved to Tottenham, in North London, I was met with a surprise. Unlike our first congregation, this church had been established for a very long time. Since 1867, when it was founded, it had seen many ministers and their spouses come and go. When we arrived, the people who held the power in this church were white and the elders among them clearly had an expectation of me as a minister's wife, which was not exactly expressed openly. As I mentioned earlier, this was not something I had spent time thinking about. The first task I was expected to fulfil was to sit on a big platform beside my husband for the formal opening of the November Bazaar, receive a bunch of flowers, and was also presumably meant to dress the part. This kind of situation was really alien to me and I hated doing it. However, the church has changed so much since that day. Again I began to carve out a ministry in this congregation using my gifts and skills among young people and children, and also initiated and developed some training. This was not what some people expected me to do, but I quietly resisted the pressure to conform to these people's expectations of me as a minister's wife. Also at this time, having been a primary school teacher previously, I now used what spare time I had to retrain and gain qualifications and training in youth and community work, youth leadership training and other related issues. I believe that through these things God enabled me to develop my ministry further.

On the family front, when we reached Tottenham our sons were aged four and one, and within two years we had fostered (long term) a daughter. During this time it was less possible for my husband to try out his sermons on me and consult me about this and that, because of the growing demands of our three children. Nevertheless he was always strong in recognizing my needs as well as his own, and our mutual support and interest in each other's work continued, but changed slightly in nature. As the children grew we continued to receive excellent support from the congregation in relation to baby/child sitting with the recognition that my mother had died a few months before moving to Tottenham, which left me with a deep feeling of loss, and that my husband's family lived a long way away.

Later on I was fortunate to gain some paid employment and also some experience in the wider Church, including the world-wide Church. During the early 1980s I became a half-time Youth Leadership Training Officer for my Synod, and full-time Youth and Children's Work Trainer in 1991. In these posts I had opportunities to develop Youth Exchange Programmes involving young people in the United Reformed Churches and those from the United Church of Jamaica and the Cayman Islands, and the Congregational and Presbyterian Churches of Guyana. Apart from this I became my denomination's representative on the Churches Commission for Racial Justice (a Commission of the Council of Churches in Britain and Ireland). I also spent six years as a commissioner on the Justice, Peace and Creation Commission of the World Council of Churches. These experiences, together with those of living and belonging to the church and community in Tottenham, helped prepare me for participating in training and education work in the field of equal opportunities, and racial justice in particular. My current half-time job that I started in 1998 has been that of co-ordinating support and training in relation to churches in urban priority areas in the London region. I also took the opportunity to work for an Open University BSc Honours degree in Social Sciences, which I am pleased to say I have achieved. All these opportunities and experiences have broadened my outlook on the world, and of this society in particular, and have developed my understanding of the pastoral demands placed on a congregation and minister within such a community as this. As well as the usual personal and social problems that impact upon people, there are further struggles, particularly for black and Asian peoples, relating to racism – particularly in employment, from the police, and the criminal justice system, and issues relating to imprisonment and immigration.

Returning to the family front once again, one of the things I began to find increasingly difficult was when my husband was wanting to share with me the pain of pastoral and church problems (except the confidential ones). I found the burden of this too much at times, with the struggles in my own job and those relating to the raising and nurturing of our children. Clearly a minister of a church needs someone on whom to off-load, but is this the role of only his wife? At one point I expressed my difficulty with this, and it was then that my husband agreed that he would find somebody outside our church situation that could take on this role and with whom he could meet at fairly regular intervals. During these meetings he could also be helped to reflect on his ministry. This has happened and is working well.

Since those early months in this congregation, the church has been transformed in so many ways, having changed beyond recognition. The group of people who held the leadership roles in the first days of our being here have either moved on to different places, or died. The leadership, including elders, pastoral helpers, youth and children's workers, hospital visitors, etc. are predominantly black Christians. This situation has helped to re-shape expectations and behaviour in relation to a variety of issues within the life of the church. For example, people whose early spiritual formation took place in the Caribbean or Africa have brought their own particular understandings and expectations of ministry and roles, including that of a minister's wife. From time to time I am teased with the words 'You are not a traditional minister's wife' or I hear humorous comments about the fact that I don't bake cakes or do gardening like the last minister's wife. However, I actually feel that the congregation, and particularly other parents, value the ministry I exercise in the church which I see myself doing as a church member. I know that there is a very small minority who find it difficult to come to terms with the fact that I do not always dress in the way some would like. I never wear hats and rarely wear skirts! When I have, someone has commented 'Oh, you have legs?' Occasionally a person has commented when I have not attended every adult-orientated activity of the church. Instead of struggling to always try to please other people, if I sense there is a problem here I usually explain to people that I am either at work or I have been spending time with youth activities or their leaders in the youth and children's programmes of the church. In explaining what I do, it is not so much a justification – but I believe it helps each of us to understand more about the total life of the Church, seeing her as the Body of Christ, a body to which people of different ages, abilities and ethnicities can contribute and carry our their different functions.

I find the words from 1 Corinthians 12:13 (NIV) helpful here. Reflecting on this image of the Church, I do not find any justification or evidence for anyone to be put on a pedestal, whether it be the role of a minister's wife or any other role. Certainly in the list of roles and functions that St Paul has mentioned for us to carry out in the Church (1 Corinthians 12:28), I do not see the mention of ministers' wives. The roles and functions that are listed here are apostles, prophets, teachers, healers, pastoral carers and administrators. We are also reminded in the following chapter (1 Corinthians 13), that the most important things to focus on are faith, hope and love, but the greatest of them all is love. My understanding here is that all of us who are Christians need to be focusing on the roles and functions which help to build up the Church, the Body of Christ, so that God's love can permeate through the Body, interacting in creative and healing ways with individuals, groups, communities and nations. Emphasizing traditional and cultural expectations of roles such as that of a minister's wife can be a diversion from our main focus as Christ's Church. In recent years, the ministry that has developed for me has embraced social justice concerns, and racial justice in particular. What has been increasingly important for me in the life of the Christian Church is the extent to which the Body of Christ is in solidarity with people in their struggles and joys within congregations and communities. I believe the Church needs to share in these kinds of relationships at local, regional, national and international levels, discovering ways of listening to people's pain and energy, and celebrating achievements; in fact, being and discovering Christ in the world.

As my awareness and understanding of God have grown, I have thought more about the different roles of the Church itself. It seems to me that the Body of Christ should not neglect any of its roles, because they are all important for the healthy and holistic working of the whole body. I am referring here to the servant, teaching, proclamation and prophetic roles, and the fact that if any of these are ignored or neglected then the whole body suffers and is impoverished. This results in society itself suffering, partly due to the failure of the Church to carry out these functions and responsibilities.

In relation to my own spiritual journey, as I have travelled from my first day as a minister's wife at Heaton Way Church to the present time here in Tottenham, I am thankful to God for walking alongside and working with me as I have moved in and out of so many experiences, from which I have learnt so much. I feel that these two congregations have enriched my life considerably. I celebrate the friendships, support, challenge and correction I have received from so many individuals within these churches. Some people say that ministers and their spouses should not make particular friends with people in the church. I can't imagine how lonely and isolated I would have been if I had not formed friendships within the churches. Friendships have always formed a significant part of my journey and I guess they will continue to do so. I am not aware that this has ever caused any problems in either congregation.

Friendship seemed to be an important hallmark in Jesus' relationships with, and between, his disciples. Without friendship there would be a kind of empty coldness. As my husband and I have developed spiritually and in our faith we have learnt more effectively how to work on issues and activities together. Clearly we have discovered what we can work on together and what we can't. Although we have a similar ethos and vision, we have different methodological approaches to things. This could cause friction in some instances, so we avoid working together in such situations. One of the creative activities we have worked well together with, has been the residential youth weeks away when we have run a programme with young people from our church and neighbouring churches, in centres in Devon, Cornwall, Wales, and elsewhere.

I have also reached a stage of confidence in being able to explain to the congregation, through groups and individuals, how Francis and I work best and to be clear about saying 'Yes' and 'No' to requests and expectations. I hope the two of us will continue to be supportive to each other in our respective ministries, be there for one another and continue to create an environment within our home, contributed to greatly by our older children, where others can feel welcome, share problems and joys in a relaxed atmosphere. We also want it to be a space for praying, singing, eating and drinking and where a young person can spend a few nights if they are shut out of their home or had a temporary upset with parents, or just come and play computer games and watch TV.

In conclusion, I would like to say that, in relation to church congregations, I feel they need to think and act carefully and sensitively regarding expectations placed on ministers' wives. Hopefully there will be a recognition that ministers' wives come with different backgrounds, experiences and skills. For example, I grew up in a nuclear and extended family that had no relationship with the Church except for 'hatch', 'match' and 'despatch' (christenings, weddings and funerals as they were called). I was sent to church with a neighbour when I was six years old. Through my childhood and adolescence I became very involved in my local Congregational Church and in the Girls' Brigade at the Baptist Church. When I was 21, my mother became a committed Christian and a member of the Church. As I grew up I did not have much knowledge about how ministers' or church families operated. Also, it is important to remember that when a man and woman marry, they marry one another, not the

Church. It is now common for men and women to enter the ordained ministry at different stages in the life-cycle, and in many situations a couple could have been married for a long time before one of them enters the ordained ministry, and therefore life and work patterns would already have been established. Hopefully the spouse of the minister would share in his/her vision and give support. In terms of the role of the spouse, in this case a wife, I believe there should be choices and that these should be respected. For example, there is one school of thought that the role of a minister's wife is to dedicate most of her life to serving her husband and staying at home all the time. Any aspirations she may have of developing her own skills and ministry is not even considered and certainly would take second place. This idea, that woman is there to serve man, smacks of patriarchy, in that man comes first, and women and children second. Although society and the Church would claim otherwise, there are strands of both that continue to hang on to patriarchy. However, if a minister's wife chooses to take on this role and feels comfortable doing this, then she should be free to follow this road. The problem for her is when she feels pushed into that role either by her husband or the congregation. Equally, if the wife chooses to develop her skills and ministry as a church member in her own right, or even a career outside the Church, she should be encouraged to do so. As Christians we need to be encouraging one another in the things that help us develop as persons, reaching out to our full potential in God.

I believe that particular expectations of the role of a minister's wife belong more in the realm of church traditions and a culture that has been built up around these traditions, rather than belonging to the arena of faith and scripture. We need to be constantly questioning this realm lest we end up, like the Pharisees, in adding all kinds of expectations and rules to peoples' lives that result in weighing us down and oppressing us, rather than liberating us to be the people God wants us to be.

Finally, returning to myself, I would ask the question as to whether being a minister's wife has made any difference to the range of experiences and work I have been able to engage in. Has being a minister's wife made access into my churches and congregations and the wider Church easier, and so facilitated my involvement with different arenas of church life, or would I have ended up doing similar ministries because of the kind of person I am, and have become? I am reminded that each of us, and the person next to us, can never fully be understood. Each of us is more than a description or explanation. Each of us is a unique world of experience and mystery, so I guess I shall never know the answer to that question. However, I am thankful to God for all the life opportunities I have had and am having in my various roles and responsibilities, struggles and joys in relation to being a wife, a mother, a Christian, and a worker.

THE BIBLE AS A TOOL FOR GROWTH FOR BLACK WOMEN

Hyacinth Sweeney

Hyacinth Sweeney is a Caribbean British woman from Slough, England. She studied her Masters in Theology at the University of Birmingham. This paper forms part of her dissertation on 'Black Women and Tools of Empowerment'. She plans to continue with her research within this challenging field, drawing together previous work that focused on 'Black Women in the Bible as a Liberative Tool'.

The Bible is not a closed book that has already said all that needs to be said. It is a collection of texts that can speak to everyone in many different ways if we take our time to be open to it. It is a text that can speak to us in our present times about things that have gone by, the things of now and the things to come. Throughout the course of biblical studies, black scholars have sought to understand the realities of the Bible for black people. The Bible was used against black people as a means to justify the slave trade and slavery. It was used against them to keep them submissive and subhuman. Despite this there are many thousands of black people who live according to the Bible and its teachings. It can still be said, even today as we move into the twenty-first century, that most African Caribbean households, in Britain and the Caribbean, still have a Bible somewhere in the house. It may not be used as much today as before, but it is the one book that will be turned to in a time of need.

Within most households you will find that it is the woman who does most of the teaching and nurturing. This is usually due to the fact that they spend most of the time with the children. The mother or grandmother will take the children to church, and be the one who helps them with the memory verse for next week's Sunday School. When the children get to a certain age, usually around teenage, they make a decision whether or not to continue going to church. Their choice depends upon what is going on around them: peer pressure, family and friends. If, however, they choose to reduce their attendance at church, this does not usually mean that they also abandon the teaching that they have received. The Bible is still the book that is turned to when 'trouble comes calling'.

In this paper I will be focusing on the four approaches that are used by womanist theologians to read the Bible. As most of the data comes from the African American contexts, I have used the data gathered from the questionnaires/interviews to get a black British perspective. All of the approaches are based on the hermeneutical method of biblical analysis as it focuses on the experience of the people rather than theory. The main emphasis will be on the Recuperative, Suspicion, Postmodern and Survivalist approaches as tools for growth. I will be using material from Professor Renita Weems, the leading African American womanist biblical scholar's lecture, 'Reading as an Act of Rebellion' (Queen's College, Birmingham, March 1997).

When it comes to the people in the Bible, women as a whole are submissive and black women within the text are invisible. They are camouflaged in terms of country of origin or by their family name, usually their father or husband. This obscurity does not enable the reader to recognize the black women or the black family lineage. With this knowledge, black theologians, male and female, began to approach the Bible using a hermeneutical method. This approach is described by J. S. Croatto as a way of understanding the Bible through the eyes of the oppressed (1987, p. 1).

If we look at the black experience, our culture and experience shape the way that we worship God and study the Bible. Our traditions were taken from Africa up through Europe and transformed within the Caribbean and America and then distributed all over the world. Therefore our experiences, our culture, our traditions, all go together to help and shape the way we see God. Similarly, European theology was formed out of the experience and culture of the European (mainly white males). Other forms of theological discourse therefore are not a new thing, but an area that has been kept silent and invisible.

Black women began to 'come to voice' and speak out against these continual injustices which others seemed to not see or just ignore. Black theologians seemed to ignore sexism and the white feminist movement failed to address racism. Many African American women[1] began to write about their own experiences and theological analysis. They took on the term 'womanist', coined by the novelist Alice Walker (1995, pp. xi–xii), and began to call themselves womanist theologians. Their work takes seriously the experience of black women and men, focusing on how this experience affects the construction and production of their lives. Experience is the key element within this discourse due to the fact that black women are seen to be suffering from multidimensional oppression, e.g. sexism, classism, racism, heterosexism/homophobia.

First, the Recuperative approach. This method sees finding black women within biblical texts as imperative. This approach enables black women to reclaim their historical presence which tradition had either camouflaged or made invisible. It takes the viewpoint that there is evidence of black women within the Bible and we must claim back our heritage. This approach reclaims the role and the identity of black women and black people within the Bible. Evidencing them within various texts, as well as heightening their contributions through history, for example, within the biblical narratives and their relationship with God; and through their expression, experiences, spiritualization, theological understanding alongside the portrayal of Jesus.

The Bible is an Eastern document in origin, and is based in a part of the world where the dominant culture is black. For example, within the Bible you have accounts of the Queen of Sheba (near Ethiopia); Moses' Cushite (Ethiopian) wife; Hagar, the Ethiopian slave woman of Sarah and Abraham, to name a few. There are many more black people within the texts that need to be identified.[2] Therefore, this approach can be seen as a positive form because it demystifies the Bible in terms of Eurocentric ideology. It places black women and men within the contexts of the pages; their life, culture and traditions are there to be seen. It is about 'claiming back', and black women need to therefore ask themselves, 'What is it that they need to claim back and how are they going to do it?' It is about gaining historical sources as a background and then moving forward towards liberation and growth.

Second, the Suspicion approach. This method approaches the Bible objectively and so makes the starting point experience. It allows us to go beyond the face value of Eurocentric biblical hermeneutic to an African-centred form. It has a strong resistance to male domination and bias, or what can be termed as 'anti-women', 'androcentric' in attitude and form. This usually takes the form of misinterpretation, misrepresentation, being seen as or made into a second-class role, if any role or position at all. This in turn points to the Bible as being biased towards men, i.e. it highlights the men more than the women within the text. The fact that the Bible has been written mostly by men encourages the notion of male superiority and female inferiority. This means that the texts therefore enslave women, especially black women, placing them in a multidimensional oppression. This is achieved in many ways: belittling the women by demonizing them; allowing them to remain as unnamed characters, which in turn makes them less obvious to the reader.

If we look at the account in Exodus 2:3–5 about Moses as a baby, four women were very influential in the continuation of his life: 'his mother hid him, he was watched over by his sister, rescued by the daughter of the pharaoh and her maid'. These important historical contributions by women have failed to be recognized by interpreters; or maybe it was a deliberate act to divorce and deny the importance of the role of women. With this approach you learn to re-read the Bible in a new form, as an act of rebellion.

Third, the Postmodernist approach. Within this method the Bible is rejected as a collection of stories that have successfully kept black women in their place, through a maintenance of certain power relationships. Women have looked beyond the male centredness of scriptures and have shown themselves to be approved by God. However, within this approach there are many who have rejected the Bible altogether, as they view it as serving male interests only.[3] These women look for answers outside of the Bible as they see God's relationship with women as an abusive one, as in Hosea 2:10 and Haggai. Also within this approach you would bypass the biblical narratives in order to use experience and modern-day concepts as tools. This approach draws on resources outside the Bible to enhance the plurality and cohesion of the texts along with our life experiences.

Howard Thurman, in his biography, tells the story of his grandmother's listening habits. She was raised in the period of slavery in America, and particularly depended upon memory and listening to grapple with and to interpret the Bible. Thurman writes:

Two or three times a week I read the Bible aloud to her. I was deeply impressed by the fact that she was most particular about the choice of scriptures. For instance, I might read many of the more devotional psalms, the gospel again and again, but the Pauline Epistles never, except at long intervals, the 13th chapter of 1st Corinthians. With a feeling of great temerity, I asked her one day why it was that she would not let me read any of the Pauline letters. What she told me I shall never forget. During the days of slavery she said, the master's minister would occasionally hold services for the slaves. Old man McGhee was so mean; he wouldn't let a Negro minister preach to his slaves. Always the white minister used as his text, something from Paul, and at least three or four times he used as his text, 'Slaves be obedient to them that are your master . . . as unto Christ'. Then he would go on to show how it was God's will that we were slaves and how if we were happy slaves, God would bless us. I promised my maker that if I ever learned to read, and if freedom ever came, I would not read that part of the Bible. (Thurman, 1949, pp. 30–1)

The grandma presumably never learned to read the Bible for herself and needed her grandson to read for her. Because of her aural contact with the Bible, it left her free to criticize and reject those portions and interpretations of the Bible that she felt insulted her innate sense of dignity as an African, a woman, and a human being. Likewise she felt free to cling to those that she viewed as offering her inspiration as an enslaved woman and had portrayed, in her estimation, a God worth believing in. Her experience of reality became the norm for evaluating the contents of the Bible. That grandmother's refusal to have the Pauline portions of the Bible read to her highlights important ways in which the experience of oppression has influenced women's, particularly African American women's, disposition toward reading the Bible.[4]

Fourth, the Survivalist approach. This method adopts a 'by any means necessary' approach. The starting point can include any of the above methods as the emphasis is placed on the liberation rather than application. This method incorporates the interpretation of the Bible in such a way as to enable it to come alive in a liberative form. This is accomplished by looking beyond the male-orientated text and the frailty of human beings and seeing God's liberating power for women. This approach esteems the value of womanhood and raises the level at which it is perceived, thereby revealing God as non-partial.[5]

Womanist biblical theologian Dolores Williams looks at the story of Hagar and uses her encounter to express the issues of survivalism within the African American women's experience. It is a story familiar and even haunting for African American, Caribbean, and black British female readers (Weems, 1997). The experience of Thurman's grandmother shows that there is a history of resistance with particular African American women and women in other cultures when reading the Bible.

Professor Weems can be placed within all of the approaches, as her work not only looks at the reclaiming of the black women from within the texts in a liberative form, but also rejects those scriptures that dehumanize and misogynize women. Professor Weems asks how and why contemporary readers from marginalized communities continue to regard the Bible as a significant resource for shaping modern existence. She explores the rationale by which African American women, marginalized by gender, ethnicity and often class, continue to regard the Bible. In her attempt to develop a critical hermeneutical method for dealing with African American women's issues, she provides a model for the way in which other problematic material in the Bible (e.g. slavery, homosexuality, war, racism and classism) can therefore be assessed (Venable-Ridley, 1997).

A black British perspective

In the interview/questionnaire, I gathered data from people to ascertain their responses on tools for growth within the Bible. I addressed a number of different black women within the church, lay and ordained, at different levels. Most of the respondents agreed that the Bible in itself can be used as a tool for growth. They were all cautious about using only the Bible as a resource, as there are many other tools that can be focused on as well. They all read the Bible in different ways, but mainly as a tool of spiritual growth. They all use caution within their reading, as they see it as a book that has been used as a tool of subjugation and oppression. They see a need for the continual discovery of black women within the text, for the accounts that are popular (as mentioned above) are far and few between. The stories of the women are welcome as a tool for identification and direction, but due to the non-recognition of most of the women within the Bible, many feel angry. They see the accounts as a small oasis in an arid mass, nurturing water splashing on you when you are hot. This, however, is not enough, and they all contend that there needs to be more recognition of women in the texts.

Most felt that women did too much in church and society without recognition. Some felt that many women saw their worth measured by the work that they did, which then becomes problematic for growth. The other side of this 'giving of self' is the model that is shown to their children. Many women will sacrifice a lot for the sake of their children and this can be seen as the testimonies of black women's commitment to growth. However, the one-sidedness of this giving needs to be thoroughly addressed by the black community throughout the world.

As we can see, the approaches used are varied, according to what your experiences and needs are. However, in order to attain tools for growth, black women need to employ approaches that will negate oppressive structures and help to promote empowerment, physically, mentally and spiritually. These tools, I contend, are found within the approaches adopted by womanist theologians as they are drawn from all sections of the community of the African Diaspora.

> Heaven is looking down on me,
>   heaven is looking down on me.
> When my friends do me wrong,
>   I shake it off and go on,
>   heaven is looking down on me.
> Heaven is looking down on me,
>   heaven is looking down on me.
> When I lay awake and can't sleep
>   I see an angel at my feet,
>   heaven is looking down on me.
> Heaven is looking down on me,
>   heaven is looking down on me.
> When I'm lonely and confused
>   I know the Lord will see me through,
>   heaven is looking down on me.
> (The Canton Spirituals, 1997)

These words portray a common response of many women, especially black women. They talk about placing everything, family, friends, worries and troubles, both near and far, with God, who they believe will guide them through. This belief is embedded into their psyche and is then instilled into the next generations.

Liberation and empowerment are words which come to mind when we talk about the tools for growth for many people. Alongside this, you will also need some aids to enable you to achieve the goals that you have set for yourself, or sometimes, ones which have been set for you. For black women over the centuries the path to liberation and freedom has continually been blocked – physically through slavery, or mentally and emotionally by the language used to describe them. Either way, the struggle to shake off the shackles has been difficult and for many a sacrificial choice. One of the main problems is the invisibility and lack of women in ministerial leadership roles, and in the organizations of the Church. The Church is supposed to be the representative of Christ, whose sacrifice was (as Christians believe), for the whole of humanity.

Notes

1 The main source for womanist theological studies is found in the African American context. My research therefore is made up of most of that literature.
2 For further studies consult Randall Bailey and Jacquelyn Grant (1995) *The Recovery of Black Presence – An Interdisciplinary Exploration*, Abingdon Press.
3 See feminists Mary Daly and Daphne Hampson.
4 Professor Weems, *op. cit.*; also see C. Michelle Venable-Ridley (1997) 'Paul and the African American community', in *Embracing the Spirit* (ed. E. Townes), Orbis Press.
5 A point to bear in mind, however is that, if one is going to raise the standard of biblical interpretation for women, then the same must be carried out on an equal basis for men, especially black men.

References

The Canton Spirituals: 'Heaven is looking (down on me)' Daddy's Boys Production, 1997.
Croatto, J. (1987) *Biblical Hermeneutics: Towards a Theory of Reading as the Production of Meaning*, Maryknoll, NY: Orbis Books.
Thurman, Howard (1949) Jesus and the Disinherited, Nashville: Abingdon Press.
Venable-Ridley, C. Michelle (1997) 'Paul and the African American community', in *Embracing the Spirit* (ed. E. Townes), Orbis Press.
Walker, A. (1995) *In Search of our Mother's Garden*, The Women's Press.
Weems, Renita (1997) Lecture at Queen's College, Birmingham, 'Reading as an Act of Rebellion'.

A WOMAN DESIGNED BY GOD

Muriel Mohabir

Muriel Mohabir was born in Beeston Spring, Westmoorland, Jamaica and trained as a nurse in Surrey and London. She was converted through the faithful witness of another Jamaican nurse. She met Philip for the first time at her baptism. She then received a call to full-time missionary work. She and Philip served in the Guyanas and Caribbean for nineteen years. They engaged in pioneer evangelism, church planting and training missionaries. They then returned to the UK in 1983. Since then she has partnered with her husband in pioneering work such as ACEA, Connections. She works primarily among single parents and leaders' wives and she often speaks at conferences. She is mother of six children.

In the beginning, God created woman; she was beautifully, wonderfully and fearfully made in the likeness and image of God. She is unique, special, full of much worth and inestimable value; the crown and glory of all creation, specially endowed with individuality, personhood, human dignity, intelligence and free will. She is the handiwork of a loving God: the unparalleled work of art intricate in design, of complex personality and of exquisite beauty with a predetermined purpose and fore-ordained destiny to fulfil (Proverbs 31:10; Psalms 139:13–15; Genesis 1:26–28). The original intention of God is that both man and woman be equal partners with a clear mandate to rule and reign together over all creation. It was never intended by God that the woman should be inferior to the man.

In the redemptive purposes and plan of God, the woman is just as accepted in the Beloved and given the authority/right to be a child of God, to be an heir of God and fellow-heir with Christ as any male (Ephesians 1:6; John 1:12; Romans 8:14–17). She is not a second-class citizen in the kingdom of God. In Paul's letter to the Galatian Christians he underlined that 'there is no discrimination between male and female'

(Galatians 3:28). Both man and woman are created as equal persons. Both were created in God's image and likeness. The woman is definitely not inferior or a second-class citizen, but in the eyes of God co-equal helper and partner to man. She was not a chance happening or an optional extra thrown in by God. No. Instead she is essential and crucial to the overall plan of God for humanity. God never intended that man should be alone. He created woman not as an afterthought, but even before the foundations of the world, Eve was part of the eternal plan. God knew that man is incomplete and inadequate without the woman. Adam was created according to divine design: and it was very good. Nevertheless he was not self-sufficient and complete – an essential half was missing. When God presented Eve to him, he recognized this. He said, 'This is bone of my bone and flesh of my flesh' (Genesis 2:23). Man and woman are created with physical and emotional needs. The woman was given to man because only another human being could meet these needs. It was always in the heart of God that Adam should have an Eve to share and care one for the other, the one to provide complement, companionship, and friendship to the other. One is as valuable as the other; they need each other. They were so designed. One cannot justifiably say to the other 'I have absolutely no need of you.'

Woman is neither inferior nor superior to man, but is equal in her personhood. Similar yet different. Unique yet vulnerable. Possessing multi-functional gifts and skills yet she is not unmitigated consummateness. But wait a minute. Surprise! The same is also true of the male species.

The woman of God's design is unique

Although male and female have many things in common, in many aspects they are not the same. A woman is the same as man in intelligence, ability to solve difficult problems and capacity for true spirituality. Her capability to worship and serve God in a variety of ways, and her availability to be used as a sanctified and suitable vessel is not preconditioned by her gender. Male and female have the same right and access to the grace of God. They are fellow-heirs of the grace and gift of God (1 Peter 3:7). However, we cannot ignore the reality that there are certain characteristics to a woman's personality and psyche that are peculiar to womanhood. Physically, psychologically, emotionally and sociologically she is designed to function differently. She is unique, handcrafted by the skilful and loving hands of the Master Craftsman himself. To be different is not necessarily to be wrong. The differences are meant to complement and enhance the whole. These differences do not diminish her self-worth, value or dignity. Instead they emphasize the necessity and strategic significance of the other half. As a matter of fact, you cannot be too dogmatic about male and female distinctions. Human beings are far more complex and intricate in their make-up than that. Any careful observation of male/female inter-relationship and patterns of thought and behaviour will reveal that there is an overlap. As someone said, 'there is a part of woman in every man and a part of man in every woman'. This should hardly be surprising since both male and female were created in the image of the one and only God. The difference is that certain qualities of God's nature are more pronounced in the woman and certain other qualities more pronounced in the man.

As a matter of fact, if and when the traits that are peculiar to one gender are emphatically functional in the opposite gender, not only is it unnatural but also it detracts, even distorts, the inner beauty and the original purpose of God's design and intention. It diminishes the masculinity or femininity as the case may be.

The woman according to God's design is unique in the following ways:

- Her ability to bear children.
- Possessing mother's love second only to God's love.
- Her tenderness and patience demonstrated in caring.
- Her intuition. She discerns more by her gut feeling than by cold rationalization and analysis.
- Her natural skill to nurture, train and inculcate values in the uninitiated that will determine their character. The hand that rocks the cradle rules the world.

- Her strength to bear pain, to agonize and to travail in order to bring new life to birth. Her unselfish surrender of her own joys, desires, pleasures and even her own life for the sake of others.
- While the male tends to be more aggressive the female tends to be more tender.
- While the male tends to be more rationalistic the woman tends to be more intuitive.
- While the male is paternal the woman is maternal in her instincts.
- While the male is robust and tougher, the woman is more affectionate, warm and personal.

However, it is important that we avoid generalizations and stereotypes, since all human traits can be found in both genders to some degree or another.

The woman should never be afraid or ashamed to be what God has made her to be. Your community may have cast you in a certain mould. Your cultural background may have created an image of who and what you should be. Society may have conveniently invented certain stereotypes of the woman's place and role. Your historical roots and traditions may have influenced and shaped your mindset about yourself. Whether they are right or wrong is not the issue: what really matters is God's opinion of you, not traditions, friends, culture, society or even your own past experiences. People often get it wrong anyway. The high priest was wrong about Hannah. Godly Zechariah misread the situation with Elizabeth. Even righteous Joseph misinterpreted Mary's condition. The disciples made wrong assumptions about the woman of Samaria, and the Pharisees miscalculated the grace of God towards the woman caught in the act of adultery. God sees more than just the hard facts: he sees your possibilities and potential. Do not let any person or system put you down. Rediscover who you are by returning to your origin and source – God, your creator, designer and redeemer. Dare to believe the Lord and his word above that of any other. Trust him. Listen to what he says: 'I love you with an everlasting love' (Jeremiah 31:3). Again the Lord declares, 'I know the plans I have for you, plans to prosper you and not to harm you, plans to give you hope and a future' (Jeremiah 29:11, NIV). Assert your God-given rights and pursue your potential in Christ to the maximum.

A woman designed by God is destined for the throne

A woman of God should know her origin, who she is and with what she has been blessed. Her origin is in God. She belongs to him both by the act of creation and the right of redemption. She is the blood-bought property of Christ. She is blessed with all spiritual blessings in heavenly places in Christ. She is saved, raised up and made to sit together in the heavenly places in Christ far above every principality and power, might and dominion, and every name that is named, not only in this age but that which is to come (Ephesians 1:3, 19–23, 2:4–6). A woman is given a place and position in Christ – a throne position. Woman, you are an equal citizen of God's household. Take your place boldly. Do not live below or beneath your calling in Christ. A woman of God is called to live out the daily nitty-gritty of life and face the stresses and pressures out of her throne position in Christ. She is called to reign over her circum-stances, not live under them. Like Esther you are called and specially chosen to be a woman of destiny. The future hopes and aspirations of many generations are in your hands. So come on queen; like Esther, take your place on the throne. The throne was prepared for you and you were designed for it. Your King bids you come.

A woman of God is involved in God's redemptive activity

Women always played a very significant role in the unfolding drama of redemption. Jesus included and involved them in his life and ministry. Observe carefully:

- The seed of the woman shall bruise the head of the serpent (Genesis 3:15).
- God used a woman to provide the world with a Saviour.

A virgin shall bring forth a son (Matthew 1:21; Isaiah 7:14, 9:6).

- Four women are named in the list of the genealogy of Jesus (Matthew 1).
- Jesus allowed the woman with an issue of blood to touch him (Matthew 9:20).
- Jesus allowed Mary to anoint his feet (John 12:3).
- Jesus allowed women to minister to him (Luke 8:2-3).
- Jesus taught Mary while she sat at his feet (Luke 10:38-42).
- On the morning of the resurrection, it was a woman who first received and ran with the message of the risen Lord (Matthew 28:8–10).

There is no record of a woman ever speaking against Jesus. Woman, you are unique and special to Jesus. So rise up and take your place.

The woman of God is blessed with the most noble of all tasks

The woman is specially designed biologically, psychologically, emotionally and sociologically to be a wife and mother. In contemporary society the concept of being wife and mother is held by some in derision.

She is not designed merely for sexual intercourse and gratification. To think of the woman just as a mere sex object is an obscene insult to her womanhood. She is created for a far higher and greater purpose. She is not just a reproduction machine either. She was invested with innate ability and creative skills for the preservation of the human race. She is meant to be a mentor – a spiritual nurturer to instil moral foundations in order to preserve future generations. There are many sociological and cultural factors that determine behavioural patterns, but none is as powerful as the influence of the mother who gives suckle to her child. Motherhood should be highly esteemed and should never be despised. Incidentally, motherhood is not a curse. God blessed Eve and commanded her to multiply long before the Fall.

However, it must be emphasized that unmarried/single women are not second-class. On the contrary, there are many other equally important, significant and necessary functions that are appropriate and applicable to womanhood. The callings, gifting and ministries of God are not restricted to married women only. As a matter of fact, Paul said that the single woman could devote herself to serve the Lord more effectively and fully (1 Corinthians 7).

The role of the woman should never be limited to domestic chores – she is far more richly endowed and valuable than that. According to Proverbs 31, the functions of a good and godly woman are diverse and many. Her role can extend to being a manager, industrialist, strategist, commercialist, financier and many others. Add to that list the 27 different gifts and service functions in spiritual ministry listed in the New Testament. Single women are blessed with the same innate qualities and traits as married women. They are blessed with as much dignity, self-worth, individuality and personhood as any other. Singles should not be alienated or despised, but instead should be appreciated and encouraged to fulfil their calling and destiny.

Woman's responsibilities at home

Let us start at home. The home provides a context for all the innate creativity and artistic skills that are peculiar to women. They can be expressed to create a secure and loving atmosphere to enable healthy and happy growth. The woman can release her warmth and energies to construct an environment where character can be developed and gifts and skills can be cultivated.

A woman's place in the home is not to be underestimated. She should see her role as God-given and seek to fulfil that role in a godly and Christlike manner (Titus 2:3–5). Although the man is head and priest of the home, it is the woman's responsibility to manage the home in consultation with and under the covering of her husband. As the saying goes, every head needs a neck to rest on and 'turn it'. If this is done in a meek and submissive spirit, love and harmony should ensue, thus creating a very loving and secure environment.

This requires much faith and prayer. The faithful prayers and tears of a godly mother never fall to the ground unanswered. God lends his ears to the heart-cry of a mother. To live a godly and Christlike life it is important to implicitly trust in the Lord and obey his word, especially when things are difficult. The life of the woman in her home should bring honour and glory to God, difficult though it may be to strive always to maintain your equilibrium in God. Do not allow circumstances, children, husband, other people or the devil to disturb your peace in Christ or to steal your joy in the Spirit. Be an example to others. In order to live in a godly way and command respect she must strive to live a Spirit-filled and Spirit-controlled life. Take time to wait in God's presence until you feel the warmth of his love, soothing your nerves and calming your fears. Listen to his voice and be quick to obey his command. Even if things become difficult in the home, do not panic, become downhearted, or give up. Instead of becoming negative, draw near to the Father. He will comfort and strengthen you and work on your behalf. Do not try to fight your battles in your own strength: allow the Lord to fight for you.

It is unthinkable that even in this highly sophisticated society, many women and children suffer all kinds of horrible verbal, emotional and physical abuse. Sometimes the assault on your soul is more subtle than these. Lack of communication, being taken for granted, loneliness, neglect and lack of appreciation inflict hurts, cause pain and tears. You may even feel bitter and distressed to the degree that you find it nigh impossible to forgive. The burdens are so heavy and the wounds so deep that you either fall into deep despair or resign yourself to endure it as your lot in life. The devil may even succeed to make you blame yourself. How should the woman of God cope with this? Remember you were not designed for this. You are destined to sit on the throne. Come to the cross, commit your burdens to the Lord and allow him to work for you. Let him fill you, refresh and re-energize you. The woman whose life is controlled by the Holy Spirit will be able to rise above adversity and go on in victory. For greater is he (Jesus) who is in you than he who is the world (1 John 4:4).

The woman of God maintains personal victory

Abigail is a beautiful example of a woman who maintained her cool and rose above a very awkward situation despite her husband's failures (1 Samuel 25:3). Abigail was married to the wealthy Nabal. He was an arrogant, surly and mean husband. David, who was anointed to be the future king of Israel, came seeking help but he was aggressive and insulting. In order to avoid the wrath of the king, Abigail acted decisively, boldly and wisely, yet humbly. She offered David and his men hospitality. In doing so she saved the lives of her entire household. She acted against her husband's wishes; but her wisdom averted a major catastrophe and even saved Nabal from destruction. Abigail, the godly and intelligent housewife, prevented a grave crisis and saved her household. David blessed and commended her for her brave and courageous actions and made her his wife after Nabal's death.

The woman of God fights for her children

Here is an example of how a woman can manage her household well in spite of a surly and mean husband. Maintaining one's spiritual life is very important and no one else can do this for you: it is a personal matter. We are called to be overcomers in spite of the impossible situations we have to face. Every woman should set a godly example for her children and grandchildren. A life of true spirituality is an eternal investment in their future. Every child deserves a true spiritual heritage and positive role models on which they can build and pattern their own lives. Much emphasis and focus should be placed on our children and grandchildren. The world has many sinful attractions and dangerous distractions. Let us fight for our children (Nehemiah 4:14). The woman who knows her God will perform exploits. Let us travail in prayer and fasting to break their bondages and set them free to walk in the straight and narrow (1 Samuel 1:10–15; Luke 2:36–37).

I had to learn that my husband's dedication and commitment to God and God's work does not make me a spiritual woman. My walk with God depends solely on me. I must know God for myself (Philippians 3:10). My husband has an itinerant ministry. Often this means me being at home with the children alone to keep the fires burning. I have to shoulder my fair share of responsibilities in the home and the work with which we are involved. One lesson I had to learn is to trust God for myself in every situation (1 Corinthians 10:13). The Holy Spirit is so faithful that he is always there to help, inspire and give directions. There have been times when I have been deeply hurt, misunderstood and disappointed by people from whom I least expect it. I cannot expect my husband to carry me. I have to sort out my own heart and spirit. Through the conviction and help of the Holy Spirit I am able to forgive and release it all to Jesus. One cannot afford to harbour hurts, bitterness, unforgiveness and grudges – these things only rob us of our fellowship with the Father. The Holy Spirit's presence is precious, and I am learning more and more how to abide in his presence. Nothing is too difficult when he is in control.

Woman is called to many other functions outside the confines of the home. A woman must be confident and obedient to God's calling. At times she may feel confined to home and family, but God has given other gifts and talents. While I do not want to play down the role in the home, I would however emphasize that God has ordained and appointed women more gifts and functions to benefit the whole Body. Jesus and Paul included women in their teams. Women should be released and encouraged to explore their full potential. As members of the Body of Christ each one of us has a function (1 Corinthians 12:18). It is essential for women to discover their place, function, gift and calling. God our Father deals with us as individuals according to our specific situation, gifting and need.

Woman, discover your calling

There are two types of calling: a *general* calling and a *specific* calling:

General
We are all called to:

- live holy lives (1 Thessalonians 3:13);
- fullness in God (Ephesians 3:19);
- freedom, not bondage (Galatians 5:13);
- liberty, not legalism (2 Corinthians 3:18);
- build the right kind of relationships (Ephesians 4:14–15);
- love one another (John 15:12. This is a new commandment – 1 Corinthians 13, John 13:39);
- share Jesus' love with others (John 4:29; Acts 1:8);
- live a victorious life (1 Corinthians 15:57–58; Romans 8:37);
- be filled with the Spirit (Acts 1:8);
- pray and intercede (Luke 18:1);
- exercise at least one of the nine gifts of the Spirit (1 Corinthians 12:7, 11).

Specific

God gives specific gifts and tasks to each of us in the Body and these should function within the Body for the benefit of the Body (1 Corinthians 12:18–20). These are the five ministry gifts.

1. Apostles.
2. Prophets.
3. Teachers.
4. Evangelists.
5. Pastors. (Ephesians 4:11)

Gifts of the Spirit (1 Corinthians 12:1–11) are: wisdom, knowledge, faith, healing, interpretation, miracles, discernment, tongues, helps. There are other useful giftings that can be used effectively. Administrative gifts (1 Corinthians 12:28) are: administrators, secretaries, co-ordinators, intercessors, mothers, children's workers, youth workers, encouragers. Earnestly covet the gifts.

Woman of God – role model

Examples of some women who are outstanding role models:

- *Esther:* she was chosen to bring deliverance to her people (Esther 2).

- *Deborah:* prophetess and judge, she judged Israel and gave leadership for years through a very difficult period of their history (Judges 4).
- *Mary:* mother of Jesus, was specially chosen ('Hail, favoured one, the Lord is with you.') What an honour that a woman is chosen to bring forth the Son of God – Saviour, Messiah and redeemer (Luke 1:28).
- *Anna:* intercessor and prophetess known for her faithfulness (Luke 2:36–37).
- *Samaritan Woman:* after she met Jesus she became a faithful witness and led a whole city to come and meet Christ (John 4:29).
- *Dorcas:* abounding with deeds of charity (Acts 9:36).
- *Lydia:* worshipper of God and a woman of prayer (Acts 16:14).
- *Priscilla:* trusted fellow-worker with Paul (Acts 18:18–19).

See also the list of women in 1 Corinthians 16 and Romans 16.

Throughout the scriptures, both in the Old and New Testaments, women played prominent roles. God can use any woman who makes herself available. God has a plan for your life: find it.

Woman, take your place

God is calling on women to take their rightful place and to be faithful. To fulfil God's calling effectively, the anointing of the Holy Spirit is needed. He alone can give us:

- Divine energy (Acts 1:8; Acts 10:38; Joel 2:28);
- Divine equipment (1 Corinthians 12);
- Divine enablement (Zechariah 4:6).

- *Divine energy:* God anointed Jesus of Nazareth with the Holy Spirit and power. The anointing is the overflow of God's energy in our lives and we need to be always conscious of his presence with us (John 14:16; Joel 2:28), and of the promise of the outpouring of the Holy Spirit on mankind, our sons and daughters.

- *Divine equipment:* (1 Corinthians 12): Only the Holy Spirit can equip us. Although there are different gifts, all must work through the Holy Spirit. The gifts of the Spirit are given to equip us for the work.
- *Divine enablement:* (Zechariah 4:6): 'Not by might nor by power but by my Spirit saith the Lord of hosts.' To be effective we need the Holy Spirit's anointing. We need the anointing to wage war against principalities and powers (Ephesians 6:12).

To be an equipped woman of God, certain things need to be observed:

- The need to read and study God's word regularly.
- Pray, fast.
- Intercede.
- Seek God for his gifting.
- Step out in boldness and faith.

Hindrances

Some problems women need to release:

- *Fears* – cause torment and are from Satan.
- *Hurts* – destroys one's spirit.
- *Unbelief* – breeds doubt.
- *Bitterness* – causes unpleasantness.
- *Guilt* – brings self-condemnation.
- *Rejection* – harbours self-pity.
- *Low self-esteem* – causes an inferiority complex.
- *Negative passivity* – can lead to depression.

God can use any woman who is set free and walking in victory effectively. So arise and go forth in faith. Whatever the Father allows is for our good. '"For I know the plans that I have for you" declares the Lord, "plans for welfare and not for calamity. To give you a future and hope"' (Jeremiah 29:11).

A VIRTUOUS WOMAN IN THE TWENTY-FIRST CENTURY

Pauline Muir

Pauline Muir is married with two daughters and two stepdaughters. She attends Mile End New Testament Church of God and is a Senior Lecturer in Arts Management at the South Bank University.

A wife of noble character who can find? She is worth far more than rubies.

Her husband has full confidence in her and lacks nothing of value.

She brings him good, not harm, all the days of her life.

She selects wool and flax and works with eager hands.

She is like the merchant ships, bringing her food from afar.

She gets up while it is still dark; she provides food for her family and portions for her servant girls.

She considers a field and buys it: out of her earnings she plants a vineyard.

She sets about her work vigorously: her arms are strong for her tasks.

She sees that her trading is profitable, and her lamp does not go out at night.

In her hand she holds the distaff and grasps the spindle with her fingers.

She opens her arms to the poor and extends her hands to the needy.

When it snows, she has no fear for her household; for all of them are clothed in scarlet.

She makes coverings for her bed; she is clothed in fine linen and purple.

Her husband is respected at the city gate, where he takes his seat among the elders of the land.

She makes linen garments and sells them, and supplies the
merchants with sashes.
She is clothed with strength and dignity; she can laugh at the
days to come.
She speaks with wisdom, and faithful instruction is on her
tongue.
She watches over the affairs of her household and does not eat
the bread of idleness.
Her children arise and call her blessed: her husband also, and
he praises her:
'Many women do noble things, but you surpass them all.'
Charm is deceptive, and beauty is fleeting: but a woman who
fears the LORD is to be praised.
Give her the reward she has earned, and let her works bring
her praise at the city gate.
(Proverbs 31:10–31, NIV)

This passage of scripture is one of my favourites in the Bible, yet despite spending all of my life in church I have never heard a sermon preached on it. The portrayal of the virtuous woman as described in Proverbs 31 (some may want to refer to her as a 'Superwoman') encapsulates all the qualities and achievements many a Christian woman would like to aspire to. It would appear that she has no difficulties in balancing a host of roles and responsibilities simultaneously: she is adept at handling the children, the husband, the job, the business, the housework, the charitable works and much more. In an age when the women who want to have their cake and own the whole bakery are blamed for the demise of manhood, this woman appears to do it all and have it all. There are no dilemmas or contradictions in embracing the role of nurturer and supporter as well as businesswoman and negotiator.

The stereotype of the 'strong, black woman' is nothing new. It is she who has maintained the survival of the black race. Yet increasingly, this woman stands alone, often isolated, angry, bitter and defiant against men. Many may still echo the view that 'The black woman had gotten out of hand. She was too strong, too hard, too evil, too castrating. She got all the jobs, all the everything. The black man had never had a chance' (Wallace, 1979, p. 11).

However, the virtuous woman in her strength shares none of these characteristics. Her strength coupled with dignity appears to engender inspiration and affection in those with whom she has contact. In this chapter I would like to examine the role and characteristics of the virtuous woman and reflect on what she has to say to twenty-first-century men and women.

Proverbs 31 is an unusual chapter in Proverbs; while it follows the warnings and the series of injunctions on how one should conduct their lives outlined earlier in the book, the monologue on the characteristics of womanhood are unprecedented within this book and, indeed, within the whole Bible. The positioning of the monologue is perhaps even more unusual when one considers its place among the wisdom literature.

> The wisdom literature, taken as a whole, is the philosophical literature of the Hebrew, being concerned with the proper governance of life through an understanding of ultimate goals and general principles. (Denton, 1971, p. 205)

Herein lies a key principle – this book offers us a biblical understanding of principles on which to govern our lives. We may be fearful of the -isms – racism, sexism, heterosexism etc. We may hold dear particular politics, denominational doctrines and adhere to our own brand of cultural baggage. However, we often collude with the ideology, principles and understanding of our confusing postmodern world. It may sometimes be difficult to locate ourselves as Christians, perhaps more so as Christian women, particularly in an age when there are so many contradictory messages for women both in the world and in the Church. However, this chapter gives us a blueprint of a woman's life that is truly of great significance. This is a radical feminism based on biblical principles.

The early sections of the chapter cite a mother's instruction to her son. This includes a warning against 'loose women' and an admonishment to administer justice for the defenceless, poor and needy.

Verses 10 to 31 set out the personal specification for the woman of virtue. It is not clear from the text whether she was simply applying an impossible image for her son to seek after; after all, no woman is ever 'good enough' for a mother's son. The picture which is drawn of the virtuous woman is one which challenges the traditional view of women. She is firstly described as a noble woman. 'Nobility' as a virtue is not often associated with women, especially in regard to qualities of character. Shakespeare speaks of the noble 'Moor' in referring to Othello, and the image is conjured up of one who is excellent in mind and character.

We are further told that she brings her husband good and he has full confidence in her. Contrary to the image of the submissive helpmeet, there is a sense in which this woman contributes equally to her relationship and is in a position to take the initiative. She selects, she provides food and she makes decisions. This directly challenges the notion of the man as the provider. She does not simply cook or prepare the food; the text seems to imply her role as a financial provider. This is further confirmed by verse 16 where we read that she considers a field and buys it; and furthermore, out of her earnings she plants a vineyard. Here is a woman who is capable of making astute financial judgements. Patrick Jenkins, one-time Secretary of State for Social Services, stated that 'If God had meant women to go out to work, he would not have created two sexes' (Evans, 1982, p. 13).

Contrary to Patrick Jenkins' view, this woman works and she has the financial acumen to also invest wisely and to plan for the future. Again, these are not skills usually attributed to women. We hear more about women who are shopaholics and run up enormous credit card debts.

Her arms are strong and she works hard. She is not the weak wilting female. She plays the role of not only wife and mother but that of provider, protector and procurer. She fulfils a role in the home, but also has business affairs that take her outside of the home. In all of this activity, she has not neglected the duties of caring for her children. When we are told there are many so-called high-flying women with top jobs, unable to care for their children and do a decent day's work, it is instructive to know and to have an alternative paradigm which finds resonance and legitimacy in the Bible.

A recent 'Panorama' documentary featured working mums. The series focused on recent research which 'proved' that working mums have an inability (inherent, it seems) to carry out a worthwhile day's work and give their children the care and attention they desperately need. Working mums are repeatedly told that their children will become delinquents and drop-outs in society, they will achieve lower exam grades than their peers with mums who stay at home. They will be emotional wrecks and 'no-hopers' in society. Often if a mother wants a life aside from her children it is frowned upon, and can only be perceived as secondary. Admittedly many women have enthusiasically embraced the role of staying at home and caring for children as integral to their Christian faith. However, many others cannot adopt this role due to financial needs or because they simply do not want to. It cannot be denied that the challenges of caring for a family and developing one's self outside of that family are great. Yet we see in our virtuous woman someone who has managed to achieve a multiplicity of roles without the guilt and burdens of juggling many different responsibilities.

What of the guilt, the balancing, the wrestling, not to speak of the tiredness? The woman of virtue does everything. Paradoxically, she is indeed a modern-day superwoman, both confounding and fulfilling all of the classic stereotypes. She is the strong, all-powerful assertive businesswoman. She is also the loving wife and dedicated home-maker, perfect hostess, yet independent facilitator. What does she say to women of the twenty-first century who are often confused by the role we play both in society and in the Church, who are often filled with resentment at the duality of their roles? On one hand, women (frequently black women) are blamed for the demise of the twenty-first-century man and the feminization of the Church. We are told that because of the dominance of women in the Church our black brothers are joining the Nation of Islam where 'men are allowed to be men'. The Church, it seems, is only able to affirm masculinity at the expense of woman. Men have to rule in their homes and wear the trousers. The woman of virtue seemed not to be troubled by these issues.

The Church – both the established Church and the nonconformist Church – have always had difficulties with women, even though women have always made up the largest part of congregations, indeed have been the 'backbone of the Church'. Monica Furlong states: 'Woman is the best friend religion ever had, but religion is not the best friend woman ever had' (1988, p. 1).

There are seemingly contradictory images about women as sexual time-bombs (Furlong, 1988, p. 4) or the vessels of spiritual femininity such as resided in the Virgin Mary. Should they remain in the kitchen or should they be allowed to prophesy? Some churches have not been able to reconcile the leadership role of women over the problem of authority *vis à vis* men. In my own denomination, women are allowed to be pastors, but are not allowed to sit on the pastoral council (i.e. the decision-makers of the church). Where one congregation has made an institutional shift in the direction of 'equality' in respect of women's representation on the pastoral council, the women sit as *ex-officio* members. The Church of England has battled long and hard over the ordination of women, in fact it has caused such a serious conflict that many have left to join the Catholic Church. For centuries churches have debated over the Pauline passages in regard to head-covering, headship, silence in church, etc., but women have refused to accept the silence and the invisibility.

There has been a rise of some 65 to 95 per cent in the participation of women in the black-led church (Foster, 1992). Elaine Foster describes two pyramids which exist in black church life. The first pyramid is inverted and represents the female Church, while the upright pyramid signifies the patriarchal, leadership, priestly male model. Women, she states, run the Church, but it is also women themselves who collude with this model and avoid any area of conflict. There is an acceptance that 'If you take away the women from the Church, you wouldn't have anything left' (Foster, 1992, p. 48). She refers to this as the 'benign conspiratorial knowing'. Foster talks about how women's major participation has shaped and developed practice and worship within the black-led Church, evidenced by areas like the song service and the open sharing of testimonies: '. . . it is clear that in a very real sense the churches are the women, and the women are the churches' (1992).

In 1999 Coreen Archer was still reflecting that the 'value of women in the Church needs to be recognised and affirmed. Their role in leadership should be encouraged because they have a wealth of talent and knowledge' (Archer, 1999, p. 15).

Theressa Hoover asserts that 'To confront the inequities of women and the inequities of blacks, and to have the responsibilities of a dedication to the church, is a triple jeopardy for a black woman' (Hoover, 1979, p. 377).

Women are accused of the feminization and consequently the emasculation of the Church. Black Islam is seen to represent a stronger, more powerful, macho image for young black men (Games and Nicoll, 1998).

The God of the woman of virtue is the God of the 'can-do': 'I can do all things through Christ who gives me the strength' (Philippians 4:13). Strength in this context translates into energy. The woman of virtue confirms that it is possible to be mother, wife, professional and all the other things that Christ has called me to be through him. It is possible to balance the cares of child-rearing with the rigours of professional life and the rough-and-tumble of the business world. A woman's biology does not lessen her ability to achieve, to care and to be a dynamic individual. Nor should she be afraid of embracing these roles because of the likely impact on male partners or colleagues.

As Christian women of the twenty-first century, what can the virtuous woman say to our circumstances, lives and situation? Is it an impossible model to pursue? Or is it the case that the societal freedoms women have gained and the unprecedented strides women have taken in the twentieth century now afford opportunities and make possible the implementation and realization of the qualities exemplified in the virtuous woman? Should she be used as a rod to beat or a barometer to measure how far we are from the mark, or is this an image of what is possible when women make themselves available to the kingship and lordship of Christ?

I believe that 'I can do all things through Christ who gives me the energy.' It is in the doing of the work that the release comes. The blessings are inherent in the work. The blessing *is* the work. As we work, the Father works alongside us in our work to do his good will. We must step out of our fearful mode, the 'I can't' mode. Often societal and institutional pressures seek to undermine and debase our creative and God-given energies and skills. He has called us to be people of power, women of power: not only women who can pray and preach but women who can be women of power, run businesses, engage in professional life, raise children, love husbands and be women of virtue – women who can rise above the philosophies and ideologies of the world and be all God has called them to be.

We live in a world where people are quick to deny the power and potential, which God has invested in all of us regardless of our colour, gender or social standing. History gives us many examples of women who were able to step outside of the limits society had tried to place on them. One such woman is Sojourner Truth. She emulated many of the qualities of the virtuous woman. This remarkable woman was born into slavery around 1797. After she had secured her freedom, she spent many years campaigning for the rights of women. She prided herself on the fact that she could work as hard as any man and waged a court battle to recover her small son who had been sold into slavery. In her famous 'Ain't I a woman' speech she says:

That man over there says that women need to be helped into carriages, and lifted over ditches, and to have the best place everywhere. Nobody ever helps me into carriages, or over mud-puddles, or gives me any best place! And ain't I a woman? Look at me! Look at my arm! I have ploughed and planted, and gathered into barns, and no man could head me! And ain't I a woman? I could work as much and eat as much as a man – when I could get it – and bear the lash as well! And ain't I a woman? I have borne thirteen children, and seen most all sold off to slavery, and when I cried out with my mother's grief, none but Jesus heard me! And ain't I a woman? (Truth, 1991)

143

Her biographers document a tale which shows the remarkable power of this woman. Sojourner Truth had been on many speaking expeditions; at one such meeting it was declared by those present that she was not a woman at all, but an impostor posing as a woman. It was requested by Dr T. W. Strain that she should submit her breast for inspection to prove to the crowd that she was indeed a female. Sojourner addressed the crowd and told them that she was indeed a woman and that her breast had suckled many a white baby, many of whom were now fully grown. In disrobing herself she asked the men of the congregation if they too wished to suck! In uncovering herself she declared to the audience that the shame was not hers but theirs. Central to this woman's power and strength was her tenacious belief in God.

Another woman who exhibits many of the characteristics of the virtuous woman is Jarena Lee. William L. Andrews, editor of the book *Sisters of the Spirit* (Andrews, 1986) which gives accounts of these outstanding women, says they are all examples of female self-determination. They are examples of women who were not afraid to step outside of the traditional boundaries. Society held them in low esteem; they were, after all, black and female, the lowest of the low. They would not, indeed could not, accept the shackles placed on them and believed that God had called them to do a special work and they could preach to the nations. They refused to be limited by their biology, race or class.

Jarena Lee was born in 1783 and endured many spiritual struggles, brought even to the verge of suicide in the early years of her faith in Christ. When she first told the leader of the African Methodist Episcopal Church (AME), Richard Allen, of her belief that God had called her to preach, she was discouraged by him, being told that she could hold prayer meetings or lead the congregation in exhortation, but that preaching was not a job for a woman. However, she would not lay down the mantle and held on to her belief that God had called her to preach. Eight years after her first request she appealed to Allen a second time; on this occasion permission was granted.

She was widowed early on in her marriage and left with two small children, aged two years and six months. Despite this she started her preaching career, in the course of which she travelled over 700 miles. She joined the Anti-Slavery Society and, like Sojourner Truth, campaigned for equal rights for black people. She published her autobiography and spiritual journal *Life* in 1836 and again in 1849, and also financed the printing of her *Religious Experience* and *Journal.*

The Life of Zipha Elaw (Andrews, 1986) exhibits similar qualities and determination. She was born in about 1790 and travelled to London from the United States and preached all over England. In the foreword of her journal she writes:

> I feel that I cannot present you with a more appropriate keepsake, or a more lively memento of my Christian esteem, and affectionate desires for your progressive prosperity and perfection in the Christian calling, than the following contour portrait of my regenerated constitution – exhibiting, as did the bride of Solomon, comeliness with blackness (Song of Solomon 1:5); and, as did the apostle Paul, riches with poverty, and power in weakness. (2 Corinthians 12) (Andrews, 1986, p. 51)

She was clearly aware of her own limitations, but confident of her faith and hope in Christ, and knew without a shadow of a doubt that whatever had been placed in her would be brought to fruition.

A product perhaps of her own particular Christian age, Elaw was rather conservative in her politics. In the same foreword (Andrews, 1986, p. 52), she warns against the reading of newspapers, she rails against the evils of the 'disloyal newspaper press', which she says, is the 'scavenger of slander and the harlequin of character, the masquerade of morals, and the burlesque of religion; the proteus of sentiment and the dictionary of licentiousness, the seminary of libertines and the hot-bed of sedition'. She enjoins her flock that they are 'called to be saints and not politicians'. She says that women are formed 'by nature for subordination' and that she is 'dependent on and subject to man' and that this is the 'dictate of nature'. She justifies herself as a female preacher by saying:

It is true, that in the ordinary course of Church arrangements and order, the Apostle Paul laid it down as a rule, that females should not speak in the church, nor be suffered to teach, *but* [my italics] the Scriptures make it evident that this rule was not intended to limit the extraordinary directions of the Holy Ghost in reference to female Evangelists or oracular sisters; nor to be rigidly observed in peculiar circumstance.

Elaw was indeed extraordinary; in her journal she describes her fervent religious experiences. Her husband did not share her zeal for the things of the Gospel and urged her to give up her faith. It was not until after her husband died that she started her preaching ministry. She gave her child up to the care of a relative and travelled to the slaveholding states to preach the Gospel to both black and white despite the dangers of being kidnapped into slavery. Here again we have another example of a woman who refused to accept the restraints placed on her by society and the Church. She was not afraid to step outside of the socially accepted conventions and even her own understandings of scripture to do the will of God.

I am not implying that life for these women was easy. Neither I am implying that attempting to emulate the characteristics of the virtuous woman will be easy. I am sure that this woman and the women we have reflected on were often afraid, frustrated and beaten into the ground by their lives and circumstances. The virtuous woman encourages us in our faith to join with the songwriter and assert:

> I don't feel no ways tired,
> I've come too far from where I've started from,
> Nobody told me that the road would be easy,
> I don't believe He brought me this far to leave me.
> (unknown)

Even in our liberated twenty-first century, strong women are feared and often viewed with suspicion. We are bombarded with images of the strong iron-lady Thatcher. The term conjures an oxymoron: 'iron' and 'lady' are two terms which conflict and contradict each other, the two should not be placed side by side. Yet it would appear from the text that our virtuous woman was strong, effective and quietly powerful without undermining or belittling either the men or women in her presence. Her sexuality appears to affirm her graciousness, she is not asexual, and she is very clearly female. Her positive characteristics are clearly bound up in the fact that here is a woman who worships God – Jehovah is very clearly the centre of her joy – from him her energy, strength and self-confidence are drawn. Can Christ become the source of the twenty-first-century woman? Indeed, the virtuous woman can speak to all of us, married, single, with or without children, male and female, poor and rich, educated and uneducated. The virtuous woman inspires us to rise above the confines of our age, to step out of the limitations which are imposed externally and internally, to ascend with the risen Christ and be men and women seated in heavenly places in order that we might show the incomparable riches of his grace (Ephesians 2:6–7).

References

Andrews, William L. (ed.) (1986) *Sisters of the Spirit*, Bloomington: Indiana University Press.

Archer, Coreen (1999) 'Ladies and few gentlemen', *Focus*, August–October.

Denton, Richard (1971) 'The Proverbs', in Charles M. Laymon (ed.), *The Interpreters: One-Volume Commentary on the Bible*, Nashville and New York: Abingdon Press.

Evans, Mary (1982) *The Woman Question*, Oxford: Fontana.

Foster, Elaine (1992) 'Women and the inverted pyramid of the Black Churches in Britain', in Gita Sahgal and Nira Yuval-Davies (eds), *Refusing Holy Orders: Women and Fundamentalism in Britain*, London: Virago Press.

Furlong, Monica (1988) *Mirror to the Church*, London: SPCK.

Games, Stephen and Nicoll, Ruaridh (1998) 'Missionary men', *The Guardian*, 2 July.

Hoover, Theressa (1979) 'Black women and the churches: triple jeopardy', in Wilmore and Cone (eds) *Black Theology – A Documentary History 1966–1979*, Maryknoll, NY: Orbis Books.

Truth, Sojourner (1991) *Narrative of Sojourner Truth*, Oxford: Oxford University Press (originally published 1850).

Wallace, Michele (1979) *Black Macho and the Myth of the Superwoman*, London: John Calder.

THE STRONG BLACK WOMAN

Andrea Encinas-Meade

Andrea Encinas-Meade is a Trinidadian by birth, British by marriage and cosmopolitan by heritage. She came to study nursing in London in 1976 after briefly toying with the idea of becoming an oil-rigger. Instead she followed her love for arts and heart for social concerns which resulted in her pioneering work with her partner Revd Bazil Meade in founding the London Community Gospel Choir and its prison ministry People's Place. Many careers later, Andrea is presently the co-founder and Director of The British Gospel Arts Consortium. Andrea has been involved in the arts since age five as a dancer then singer, and now she performs poetry under the name of 'Sugarblack'. Andrea has three children, two girls and a boy, and a stepson.

On 26 August 1995 at 11.55 p.m., while struggling with the reality of being a human instead of a myth, the strong black woman passed away, without the slightest bit of fuss.

My passing away as a strong black woman actually happened earlier than that. It was during 1985 that the years of pretence came to an end. And it felt good. It was liberating, while at the same time frightening. I had tried to play by the rules but they were not designed to keep me sane. They were designed to keep me oppressed not by racism but by the sexism within my marriage and my Christianity. As much as I tried, I would never be the good little Christian wife, silent, pious, modest, in the background, pandering to my husband's needs and making a nest for my children. No, I was loud, aggressive some would say (I prefer assertive and confident), rebellious (why are forward-thinking people called rebels?), always out starting up projects or at meetings, and certainly I did not spend enough time at home, putting my babies to bed by eight.

148

She died from being called a bitch for being verbal, a feminist for being assertive and a whore for picking her own lovers.

The training of my mother still shone through and our house and garden were always spotless and always open to strangers Trinidadian-style, even when I had three children under five years old. I was 26 years old, I had read the novels, seen the TV talk shows, watched the movies and I knew that I would never be one of those complaining 'nagging' women whose homes were untidy, whose children looked unkempt and whose personal appearance was dishevelled.

Thankfully, because of the texture of my hair, my husband would never see me with curlers or that unsexy stockingnette over my head first thing in the morning. His dinner would be ready and on the table when he came home. There would frequently be a little something I picked up from the store that I thought would look great on him. Surely, it was the lack of care in all these areas that broke up marriages. Couldn't women see that if they learned to like football and cricket, have energy for sex after a hard day running after children, and cook a fabulous meal after cleaning the house, washing and ironing the clothes, and doing the shopping without a car, their marriages would be saved? I was a strong black woman and I was going to prove to all those weak women out there that they were missing the plot, they were at fault and they needed to get their act together.

She died from always lifting something from heavy boxes to refrigerators.

When things didn't quite turn out to plan, because inconveniently I got headaches and occasionally I was tired, my perfect image of marriage started unravelling. And the more I analysed the situation and questioned my own singular purpose in life, and the more I grew in my thinking, I realized that I had set myself up to fail. I made unrealistic promises to myself that I could never keep or fulfil but I was held accountable to them anyway by those around me. The struggle began when I wanted to change and move the goalposts.

After years of holding in the pain of disappointment in myself – who can you speak to about your failures when you are a person in my position? – I finally spoke and I didn't care how it would be taken but I knew that my sanity was at stake. We grow up with the lie that says we should not speak to other people about the problems in our relationship, and in believing that lie we do great damage to ourselves physically and mentally.

Medical sources say she died from natural causes, but those who knew and used her know she died from being silent when she should have been screaming, milling when she should have been raging, being sick and not wanting anyone to know because her pain might inconvenience them; an overdose of other people clinging onto her when she didn't even have enough energy for herself.

I never thought this would happen to me. My childhood and upbringing was a very privileged one. Growing up in Trinidad, daughter to an oil-man and an occupational health nurse, we were called middle class even though the life I lived was what I thought all people should be entitled to. We were neither rich nor poor but quite comfortable. My parents brought the four of us up with a sense of social responsibility, an understanding of shared humanity and generosity of spirit. They showed us good examples of how to value people regardless of who they were – in a society where class and status were king, this was a rare quality I believe.

Trinidad was at political crossroads at the time of my birth. Four years later, in 1962, we became independent from Britain. I benefited from the nationalistic endeavours from the generation past that brought Trinidad under the control of black people. I was even born in the town where the trade union movement was started, and watched the statue of Uriah Buzz Butler from Charlie King's corner where I caught my taxi to school every morning. We are a political people; politics invades and infuses our life in the Caribbean. It involves everyone, from the beggars on the street to the owners of the yachts moored at the marina. Everyone has an opinion about national and international government, and calypsos are often more informative and revealing than the news. So it was in this country of my birth that the sufferings of my people first spoke out to me.

British Petroleum owned the oil-fields where we lived and our colonialists set up a system not unlike the apartheid system in South Africa. I did not realize at that time that the colour and ethnicity of my grandparents and parents gave us the opportunities I took for granted. The Spanish blood flowed strongly in our veins and my grandparents could easily be mistaken for tanned Europeans with their straight hair and green eyes. Within the oil-camp, there were large, fully furnished houses set in landscaped grounds for senior management staff, with a club-house, library, bar, pool, tennis and squash courts and primary school. Those were for the British ex-patriots, of course. The next level of junior management staff had sports club facilities and smaller houses set on the fringe of the camp; then there were the manual staff who lived in barracks, like terraced housing. Finally the labourers lived in aluminium shacks. I remember passing them on my way to school. It has taken me a long time to realize that it was more than choice that kept people living at that level of society.

From my position of privilege on the senior management camp setting (we had thrown out the British, nationalized the oil companies and taken over the jobs), I never saw my sex or my colour as disadvantaging me. On the contrary, I was proud of my family identity, my blackness and my sexuality, and saw nothing wrong with using all that was in me to get ahead. When I came to England in 1976 and saw the dejected state of my black British peers, I was arrogant in believing that everyone else should feel the same as me and progress as I had done.

I suspect I would have been called a strong black girl in my teenage years as I spent much free time, outside school and dance classes, visiting the hospitals and orphanages, praying with old, dying people, cheering up the male paraplegics and trying to convince them and myself that it wasn't because of their disability that I wouldn't have a relationship with them. My heart cried out for children abandoned to the orphanages by parents disappointed by the results of their labour, as we read stories and played music together. The children's wards at the hospital were filled with hopeful faces with lice-ridden hair that I picked and washed, over and over again. Then there were the beggars on the street that needed feeding, and I convinced my schoolmates that I could put their pocket money to better use and started a feeding programme during my school lunch hour. And all this strength before I was even sixteen.

There was nothing in life that could faze me. My purpose in life was to give and give and give – never expecting anything back in return. I entered my adult years with the same thinking, until so exhausted that when I looked to the Church, to my friends, my husband to give something back to me, I realized no one took me seriously. I had been strong for too long.

That was a long time ago now and there have been many changes within me. If only we could change others as we change. The change that I went through redefined my strength and gave new meaning to weakness. However, the expectations of others continue to haunt me in spite of a determination not to let it matter.

It was a news article on a suicide that caught my eye as I purchased my daily ration of salted and roasted cashew nuts and carton of Ribena from the newsagent across the road. I know with my overly full figure that it should really have been plain cashews and water – in fact some would say, just water – but do I care? It was a Sunday morning and I was taking a break from my all-night stint at the office. Yes, yet another ground-breaking project! I read the headline out loud as I put my purchases on the counter. 'You are a tough cookie, you would never consider doing something like that' my newsagent friend said, referring to the newspaper article; 'only cowardly people commit suicide'. 'And why do you think I am tough?' I replied, 'is it because I am always smiling and getting along with life in a seemingly positive way?' He smiled, as we left the question hanging in the air.

I was never beaten as a child, never been sexually abused, never had to creep out of the house to go to parties, never had cause to lie to my parents. Our parents communicated with us, we had healthy debates, they treated us with respect and trusted us to make informed decisions about our life. We spoke about sex and menstruation openly, male and female alike and walked around the house naked, comfortable with our bodies and sexuality. My British peers say that I had an abnormal upbringing for a Caribbean family. So having little baggage from childhood, I expect that I should be tough. Or is it the other way around? Isn't it your adversities, your pain in life that builds your strength of character?

I am a tough cookie! I even believe it myself. Then perhaps my recent feelings of despair and of failure, failure of not being a good enough mother, wife, friend, community advocate . . . of not coping very well or progressing fast enough in this society . . . are pure fantasy. I am a tough cookie, I am not a coward and so running away from these overwhelming feelings is a non-starter. What a burden to be seen as tough, as 'having it all together'! You see, I am still dogged by my past. In spite of myself, I am seen as self-sufficient, I rarely get ill, so people continue not to take me seriously when I am tired. Instead they say to me 'We have faith in you, we know you can do it, if anybody can do it then it is you, etc., etc., etc.' In those times I needed help, not applause.

She died from the tributes of her counterparts who should have been matching her efforts instead of showering her with dead words and empty songs. She died from myths that would not allow her to show her weakness without being chastized by the lazy and the hazy. She died from being responsible, because she was the last rung of the ladder and there was no one under her she could dump on.

Hard work and I are twins. Since I have known myself I have tried to contribute positively into whatever community I have lived. Now, in my reflective years (those are the years beyond age 40), I wonder 'Have I made a difference?'. The years of community work, church work, trade union work and labouring in the field of arts has yielded a small harvest, not reciprocal, to the time, effort and sacrifice put in. My concerns refuse to be spirited away by the clichéd response about heavenly rewards.

My greatest pleasure in life has been to mother my three children, two girls and one boy. At the same time, preparing them for life in this society has also been my greatest fear. The question I ask myself is 'How do they see their roles in this society within the context of their "African-ness", their gender and faith?' How would I react if my daughter was gay and my son brought home a white woman to marry? I worry because while I believe that loving goes beyond the boundaries of race and sex (and I have to be careful here – I don't mean that I condone homosexuality), the politics that are played out in our society using race and sex to oppress and manipulate us continue to target our children. Are they astute enough, informed enough, bothered enough to see the games being played or do they just jump up and shoot the hoop? Doreen Lawrence, mother of murdered teenager Stephen Lawrence, Mrs Reel, mother of Ricky, Mrs Sylvester, mother of Roger, all have the pain to bear of bringing up children in this country, only to lose them at the hands of racists.

She died from loneliness in birthing rooms and aloneness in abortion centres. She died of shock in courtrooms where she sat alone watching her children being lynched.

As a woman, the inequalities and injustices provoked by my 'black skin' since coming to England, my 'female form' both as a size twelve and a size twenty and increasingly 'my uncompromising faith and values' and outspokenness mean that I have to be strong to survive. Strong, they call me. Hard and aggressive. Workaholic. Good parent. Loving wife. Excellent housekeeper, gardener, cleaner, cook . . . I am a strong black woman. Should I feel good about that, is it a compliment? Ever heard of a strong white woman? No! Leads me to think then that this phrase might be patronisingly oppressive (both racist and sexist) within the context it is normally used.

I want to redefine that 'strength' from the position of enduring oppression to one of overcoming oppression, so that my daughters and my sons can celebrate who they are to each other and themselves. Strong, like Yaa Asantewaa, like Harriet Tubman, like Sojourner Truth, like Dr Maya Angelou, like Sybil Phoenix, like Claudia Jones, like all those black women who have risen above the expectations of their black men and white society, to become all that God placed inside of them.

The fantasy, myth and stereotype of the strong black woman has been with us a long time, probably coming out of the era of slavery when the survival of the African race in the Diaspora depended on the cunning and foresight of the humble African mothers. In our minds we have a pre-formed image, thanks to Jewish film-makers, of a big black mama with cuddly rolls and an ample bosom, pot on the fire and a knowing smile on her round, sweat-shined face. That smile said 'Come to me, I know exactly what you need and I can fix it for you.'

I was a contemporary version of that myth, and while my 'burden' seems trivial in comparison to Harriet Tubman's and Sojourner Truth's, the myth does not die as the struggles of racism and sexism continue to enslave me.

There is a paradox here. As black women we want to embrace the myth of superwoman, as much as some of our men want to hold on to their position as studs with penile abundance and prowess. But as black women we also want to take the load off our heads and the child off our backs, to sit down for a while and be looked after without being seen as weak.

She died from pretending the life she was living was a Kodak-moment instead of the twentieth-century, post-slavery nightmare! She died in her mind, fighting life, racism and men while her body was carted away and stashed in a human warehouse for the spiritually mutilated. Sometimes she was stomped to death by racism and sexism, executed by hi-tech ignorance while she carried the family in her belly, the community on her head and the race on her back!

African American author, bell hooks, stated in her book *Ain't I A Woman*:

When feminists acknowledge in one breath that black women are victimised and in the same breath emphasise their strength, they imply that though black women are oppressed, they manage to circumvent the damaging impact of oppression by being strong – and that is simply not the case. Usually when people talk about 'strength' of black women they are referring to the way in which they perceive black women coping with oppression. They ignore the reality that to be strong in the face of oppression is not the same as overcoming oppression, that endurance is not to be confused with transformation. Frequently observers of the black female experience confuse these issues. The tendency to romanticise black female experience that began in the feminist movement was reflected in the culture as a whole. The stereotypical image of the 'strong' black woman was no longer seen as dehumanising, it became the new badge of black female glory. (hooks, 1982)

Christianity has also thrown a triple whammy into the disempowerment of women, primarily black women, as we suffer from the 'Eve complex', guilty of the sin of mankind. In the same way that Eve has never been allowed out of Eden's garden, so today black women are still doing penance for perceived sins, even though they take a different shape.

Eve, the original woman, an African, has never been forgiven by man for making a choice independent of Adam, for exercising her rights of free will. She was cursed in childbirth by God but equally redeemed by God through the child-birthing of Jesus Christ. Unfortunately, it suits man's purpose to continue to blame and hold both God and women responsible for the survival of society.

Genesis 3:12 (KJV) says, 'The woman whom thou gavest to be with me, she gave me of the tree and I did eat.' In other words, Adam is saying that if God didn't give the woman to man, there would have not been the problem of sin.

The Church has been both the vehicle for progress, growth and development for black women and for their oppression. Church was and still is school for many Caribbean women of the Windrush generation. In days past (and even in some present communities), women were not considered a priority for education, but they were encouraged to attend church. Some parents took advantage of the opportunities of mission schools, or as we call them, church schools.

Girls did not only benefit from the A, B, C and 1, 2, 3 lessons, but also received a strict ethical training based on Christian principles and values – some too high for human achievement or expectations. We allowed ourselves to be set up to fail in our strivings for perceived holiness and purity.

She died from knees pressed too close together because respect was never part of the foreplay that was being shoved at her.

Having been brought up a Roman Catholic and rebelling from a young age against third-party interference in my relationship with God, I refused to be 'confirmed' and stopped going to 'confession'. I remember thinking very strongly that I didn't need a priest to intercede on my behalf if God was out there for everyone. After trying out the cold and dreary Roman Catholic Masses in North London, a far cry from our lively folk masses in Southern Trinidad, I found my way into a Pentecostal church that was led by women.

Women ministers were a growing phenomenon within the Pentecostal churches of the late 1960s and early 1970s. Coming in fresh from the Caribbean, never questioning the role that women played in the church in Trinidad and having gone to a convent school run by nuns, women always had seemingly positive roles to play in Trinidadian society. In Britain, I soon realised that despite the 'freedom in Christ' offered by the Church, state and Pentecostals alike, women were under subjection to a male head even though they were the majority in church.

This attitude towards women ministers was based not so much on New Testament texts as on the medieval Catholic approach. Robert G. Clouse, in his introduction to *Women in Ministry* (1989), said 'the leaders of the medieval or Latin Church in the 4th century developed an understanding of ministry that borrowed heavily from the analogy of the Old Testament priesthood. The major ceremonial functions of the Church, such as serving communion, were performed only by priests.'

Consequently women were excluded from a leadership role as this enactment of the sacrifice of Christ and the ritual purity needed for participation discriminated against women who were seen to be defiled and saw themselves as unclean during their menstrual periods. Even in the modern-day Pentecostal Church where there are women leaders, the trustees, deacons, elders and communion servers are still very much male. The other women, or 'mothers' of the church as they are called, take on the caring roles. Have you ever wondered why the women are referred to as mothers while the men are the elders, not fathers?

She died from being sexually abused as a child and having to take that truth everywhere she went every day of her life, exchanging the humiliation for guilt and back again. She died from being battered by someone who claimed to love her and she allowed the battering to go on to show she loved him too.

From my observation there are many black women who are hiding out in the Church or using it as a crutch for many things. Running away from failed marriages, abusive relationships. Courting it as a companion in their singleness. Finding a refuge from society's exclusion. Busying themselves from the terrors of sexual abuse. Escaping from the harsh realities of life. Nestling in the communal bosom of other runaway sisters. There is little realness in the lives of Christian women who 'struggle' with their womanhood. I say 'struggle' because we never to seem to talk about exploring, understanding or enjoying our sexuality – we are always trying to cope with, to control it and put it under subjection, but we do not yet even know what it is. Message after message condemns our sexuality from an early age. It is little wonder that as a black community we have so many unwanted pregnancies, particularly by teenagers from church families.

She died from tolerating Mr Pitiful, just to have a man around the house. She died from the lack of orgasms because she never learned what made her body happy and no one took time to teach her. The strong black woman is dead. She died from multiple births of children she never really wanted but was forced to have by the strangling morality of those around her. She died from being a mother at fifteen and a grandmother at 30 and an ancestor at 45. She died from being dragged down and sat upon by un-evolved women posing as sisters.

The pain of being a black woman in a society which still sees me as aggressive, defensive and angry and then makes me into a sexual object leaves me in a constant state of flux. If I speak out, become successful and demand equity in the way I am being treated or in my pay packet, I am seen as 'hard nosed' and trying to imitate my male counterpart.

The resistance to being defined as simply a sexual object is not easy for the male community to embrace, especially when the definitions originate from within the ranks of women themselves. In her book *For Yourself: the Fulfilment of Female Sexuality*, Lonnie Barbach (1991) suggested that 'women could – and should assume full responsibility for their sexuality.'

The focus on the woman as a sexual object often leaves women in a vulnerable position, open to abuse and male interpretation which insists that 'no does not really mean no, and how dare she (the female) call it off when he is ready'. Black women's concern regarding men's approach to the male–female relationship is an ongoing one, not easily resolved and cannot be overcome by talk only. There has to be a real desire to understand each other, the purpose for their God-given differences and a change in the perception about the stereotypical and traditional roles played.

Much of the change has to start with black women. We are the ones who teach our sons to be sexist, then turn around and curse the black man for not respecting us as women. After twenty-odd years of observing marriage and relationships, I have recognized that the games that are played within relationships have more to do with sexual power and race politics than to do with love and respect. These games give birth to the wrong kind of strong woman. She needs to die. Quickly!

The position I am now most comfortable with as a definition of my strength, is one that has given me my freedom from pretence, my independence from expectations, my acceptance of my difference, my frankness about my vulnerability, my appreciation of my quirkiness. I am working hard, not to be self-sufficient, but to be honest about who I am, what I need and where I am at any point of this everlasting learning curve called life. Fortunately my husband and children have stayed the roller-coaster ride with me on that journey. And why not – after all, I stayed with them on theirs.

The strong silent black woman is dead

She died from asphyxiation, coughing up blood from secrets
she kept trying to burn away instead of allowing herself the
kind of nervous breakdown she was entitled to.

She died from being misinformed about her mind, her body
and the extent of her royal capabilities.

She died in bathrooms with her veins busting open with self-
hatred and neglect.

She died from hiding her real feelings until they became mon-
strously hard and bitter enough to invade her womb and
breasts like angry tumours.

She died from sacrificing herself for everybody and everything
when what she really wanted to do was to be a singer, a
dancer or some magnificent other.

She died from lies of omission because she didn't want to bring
the black man down.

She died from loving men who didn't love themselves and
could only offer her a crippled reflection.

She died from being too black and died again from not being
black enough.

She died from castration every time somebody thought of her
as only a woman or treated her like less than a man.

She died from the lies her mother told her mother and her
mother told her about life, men and racism.

She died from the punishments received from being honest
about life, racism and men.

She died from never being enough of what men wanted or
being too much for the men she wanted.

She died from raising children alone and being criticised for
not doing a complete job.

Anonymous Poet

References

Barbach, Lonnie (1991), *For Yourself: the Fulfilment of Female Sexuality*,
Mass Market Paperback.

Clouse, Robert G. and Clouse, Bonnidell (1989) *Women in Ministry*, IVP.

hooks, bell (1982) *Ain't I A Woman: Black Women and Feminism*, Pluto Press.

POETRY

Nicola Tavares-Mott (copyright)

Nicola Tavares-Mott is a 29-year-old medical doctor currently working in the field of psychiatry. Born in Britain of Jamaican parentage, she travelled widely during her formative years as a consequence of her father's work, and has lived in West Africa and North America. She has harboured a writing talent and been a Christian from an early age.

You are not enough

You are not enough, they said.
They did not say it with their mouths,
that was their perfidy,
but they said it with their indifference
and with the remits which they reserved the right
    to set for us,
we who had long ago relinquished this right
on the altar of survival.

It had in fact always been said,
to our mothers, to our fathers
who in turn said it to us, because they had no other
    legacy of words
it became our heresy in absurd desires and concepts,
shaping even our genetic motivations
away from the natural,
becoming so powerful
only because we began to say it with our own mouths
and think it with our own thoughts,
until it entered the reservoir of things we just knew
but could not recall ever having learned.

The scar at the side of my neck

The scar at the side of my neck,
a pink flag in a chocolate sky,
exiguous but conspicuous,
begging an answer to the question – why
it's so important
to eradicate all the funkiness,
every deviation from the straight line,
the main line, the everything's fine line,
if you look like this.

Shall I compare a strand of hair to my life,
walked on a tightrope through a sea of pink flags
representing alien lands in which I have lived
as both a native and a stranger,
never forsaking my mainframe,
always appearing to play the main game,
avoiding defunking, debunking, by stealth
maintaining a certain seditionary health
negotiating a double reality by focusing on the totality
of the only one that's real; knowing that the deal
is to reach the end without falling off the rope,
to appear to bend without losing scope,
to smell the fire, but not inhale the smoke,
to remember that my face is me, and the mask is just that,
a mask – a fitting task for a true survivor.

Only those who remember to distinguish
the mask from their own face,
the shape they've assumed from the predetermined
    space,
will reach the end intact.
which I have . . .
except for the scar at the side of my neck,
a pink flag in a chocolate sky,

a war wound, a death mark if you will,
testament that in spite of my aforementioned skill,
I could not avoid killing my hair.

Summer

Summer came, early, and stole our attention
blandishing us to abandon convention,
too guileless and green to harness
convection, between two hearts,
fired by a generator a million miles away
and I speak not of the sun

Sweet as cane liquor
but fragile as a geisha's face,
it flickered and slid away,
protesting as it went
like a small child defying sleep
before the end of the world.

Not because it was not robust,
but because it could not trust
us as containers was it unable
to repel the ensuing autumn,
but you can still trace the wet mascara down my cheek
to winter, where, funnily enough
organic things survive,
under the ice.

Thoughts for friends

If you were to have thoughts for friends,
fantasy for company neurochemical circuitry
providing liminality instead of sanity,
Would you, like me, spend an eternity
envisioning clemency to soothe your history,

ploughing synaptic routes
in search of truths more bearable than truth?

If you were to have thoughts for friends,
fantasy for company neurochemical circuitry
duplicating reality – (wasn't meant to be except she
    performed perfidy),
Would you, like me, live in a wilderness with its own
    soapbeat,
and no limitations
roamed by renegade ruminations,
deferential only to potential,
paying no homage to certainty,
freeing me from odds which browbeat?

Howbeit Hollywood has nothing on this?

Tension

Round and round the room I go
Round and round my mind I go
Why does he . . . ?
How do I
go on?, when the tension in my mind winds
like a bobbin, set tight, thread pulling
arm rising, falling. Will it snap?
Will it hold?

              I thought he told me I'm The One
                  Last night, this morning
                        Hit, miss
                  Embrace, refrain
                       Kiss, diss
           Strain, draining my elixir
                   How to fix her?
                Rehearse the drill
                Rehearse the drill